MW00791297

LIGUORI CATHOLIC BIBLE STUDY

# Prophets I

## ISAIAH, JEREMIAH, LAMENTATIONS, BARUCH

## WILLIAM A. ANDERSON, DMIN, PHD

Liguori
LIGUORI, MISSOURI

Imprimi Potest:
Harry Grile, CSsR, Provincial
Denver Province, The Redemptorists

Printed with Ecclesiastical Permission and Approved for Private or Instructional Use

Nihil Obstat: Rev. Msgr. Kevin Michael Quirk, JCD, JV
    *Censor Librorum*

Imprimatur: + Michael J. Bransfield
        Bishop of Wheeling-Charleston [West Virginia]
        September 1, 2013

Published by Liguori Publications
Liguori, Missouri 63057

To order, call 800-325-9521
www.liguori.org

**Library of Congress Cataloging-in-Publication Data**

Anderson, William Angor, 1937-
    Prophets I : Isaiah, Jeremiah, Lamentations, Baruch / William A. Anderson, DMin, PhD.
    pages cm
1. Bible. Isaiah—Textbooks. 2. Bible. Jeremiah—Textbooks. I. Title.
    BS1515.55.A53 2014
    224'.0071—dc23

                                                            2013044734

p ISBN: 978-0-7648-2135-6
e ISBN: 978-0-7648-6922-8

Liguori Publications, a nonprofit corporation, is an apostolate of The Redemptorists. To learn more about The Redemptorists, visit Redemptorists.com.

Printed in the United States of America
18 16 15 14 13 / 5 4 3 2 1
First Edition

# Contents

**Dedication 5**

**Acknowledgments 6**

**About the Author 6**

**Introduction to *Liguori Catholic Bible Study* 7**

***Lectio Divina* (Sacred Reading) 9**

**How to Use This Bible-Study Companion 12**
  *A Process for Sacred Reading 13*
  *Group-Study Formats 14*

**Introduction: Prophets I 17**

**Lesson 1   The Book of Isaiah (I) 20**
  *Group Study (Isaiah 1—5) 21*

**Lesson 2   The Book of Isaiah (II) 29**
  *Part 1: Group Study (Isaiah 6—9:6) 30*
  *Part 2: Individual Study (Isaiah 9:7—39:8) 35*

**Lesson 3   The Book of Isaiah (III) 50**
  *Part 1: Group Study (Isaiah 40—42) 51*
  *Part 2: Individual Study (Isaiah 43—55 ) 54*

NOTE: The length of each Bible section varies. Group leaders should combine sections as needed to fit the number of sessions in their program.

**Lesson 4   The Book of Isaiah (IV) 66**
*Part 1: Group Study (Isaiah 56—58) 67*
*Part 2: Individual Study (Isaiah 59—66) 70*

**Lesson 5   The Book of Jeremiah (I) 79**
*Part 1: Group Study (Jeremiah 1—2) 79*
*Part 2: Individual Study (Jeremiah 3—20) 83*

**Lesson 6   The Book of Jeremiah (II) 99**
*Part 1: Group Study (Jeremiah 21—23:8) 100*
*Part 2: Individual Study (Jeremiah 23:9—35:19) 103*

**Lesson 7   The Book of Jeremiah (III) 114**
*Part 1: Group Study (Jeremiah 36—38) 115*
*Part 2: Individual Study (Jeremiah 39—52) 119*

**Lesson 8   The Books of Lamentations and Baruch 131**
*Part 1: Group Study (Lamentations 1—2) 132*
*Part 2: Individual Study (Lamentations 3—5; Baruch 1—6) 135*

# Dedication

This series is lovingly dedicated to the memory of my parents, Angor and Kathleen Anderson, in gratitude for all they shared with all who knew them, especially my siblings and me.

# Acknowledgments

Bible studies and reflections depend on the help of others who read the manuscript and make suggestions. I am especially indebted to Sister Anne Francis Bartus, CSJ, DMin, whose vast experience and knowledge were very helpful in bringing this series to its final form.

## ABOUT THE AUTHOR

**William A. Anderson, DMin, PhD,** is a presbyter of the diocese of Wheeling-Charleston, West Virginia. A director of retreats and parish missions, professor, catechist, spiritual director, and a former pastor, he has written extensively on pastoral, spiritual, and religious subjects. Father Anderson earned his doctor of ministry degree from St. Mary's Seminary & University in Baltimore, and his doctorate in sacred theology from Duquesne University in Pittsburgh.

# Introduction to
## *Liguori Catholic Bible Study*

READING THE BIBLE can be daunting. It's a complex book, and many a person of goodwill has tried to read the Bible and ended up putting it down in utter confusion. It helps to have a companion, and *Liguori Catholic Bible Study* is a solid one. Over the course of this series, you'll learn about biblical messages, themes, personalities, and events and understand how the books of the Bible rose out of the need to address new situations.

Across the centuries, people of faith have asked, "Where is God in this moment?" Millions of Catholics look to the Bible for encouragement in their journey of faith. Wisdom teaches us not to undertake Bible study alone, disconnected from the Church that was given Scripture to share and treasure. When used as a source of prayer and thoughtful reflection, the Bible comes alive.

Your choice of a Bible-study program should be dictated by what you want to get out of it. One goal of *Liguori Catholic Bible Study* is to give readers greater familiarity with the Bible's structure, themes, personalities, and messages. But that's not enough. This program will also teach you to use Scripture in your prayer. God's message is as compelling and urgent today as ever, but we get only part of the message when it's memorized and stuck in our heads. It's meant for the entire person—physical, emotional, and spiritual.

We're baptized into life with Christ, and we're called to live more fully with Christ today as we practice the values of justice, peace, forgiveness, and community. God's new covenant was written on the hearts of the people of Israel; we, their spiritual descendants, are loved that intimately by God today. *Liguori Catholic Bible Study* will draw you closer to God, in

## Group and Individual Study

*Liguori Catholic Bible Study* is intended for group and individual study and prayer. This series gives you the tools to start a study group. Gathering two or three people in a home or announcing the meeting of a Bible-study group in a parish or community can bring surprising results. Each lesson in this series contains a section to help groups study, reflect, pray, and share biblical reflections. Except for Lesson 1, each lesson also has a second section for individual study.

Many people who want to learn more about the Bible don't know where to begin. This series gives them a place to start and helps them continue until they're familiar with all the books of the Bible.

Bible study can be a lifelong project, always enriching those who wish to be faithful to God's Word. When people complete a study of the whole Bible, they can begin again, making new discoveries with each new adventure into the Word of God.

# Lectio Divina
# (Sacred Reading)

BIBLE STUDY isn't just a matter of gaining intellectual knowledge of the Bible; it's also about gaining a greater understanding of God's love and concern for creation. The purpose of reading and knowing the Bible is to enrich our relationship with God. God loves us and gave us the Bible to illustrate that love. Pope Francis stressed in an address April 12, 2013, "The Church's life and mission are founded on the Word of God, which is the soul of theology and at the same time inspires the whole of Christian life." A study of the Bible is not only an intellectual pursuit but also a spiritual adventure that should influence our dealings with God and neighbor.

## The Meaning of *Lectio Divina*

*Lectio divina* is a Latin expression that means "divine or sacred reading." The process for *lectio divina* consists of Scripture readings, reflection, and prayer. Many clergy, religious, and laity use *lectio divina* in their daily spiritual reading to develop a closer and more loving relationship with God. Learning about Scripture has as its purpose the living of its message, which demands a period of reflection on the Scripture passages.

## Prayer and *Lectio Divina*

Prayer is a necessary element for the practice of *lectio divina*. The entire process of reading and reflecting is a prayer. It's not merely an intellectual pursuit; it's also a spiritual one. Page 16 includes an opening prayer for gathering one's thoughts before moving on to the passages in each section. This prayer may be used privately or in a group. For those who use the book for daily spiritual reading, the prayer for each section may be repeated each day. Some may wish to keep a journal of each day's meditation.

## Pondering the Word of God

*Lectio divina* is the ancient Christian spiritual practice of reading the holy Scriptures with intentionality and devotion. This practice helps Christians center themselves and descend to the level of the heart to enter an inner quiet space, finding God.

This sacred reading is distinct from reading for knowledge or information, and it's more than the pious practice of spiritual reading. It is the practice of opening ourselves to the action and inspiration of the Holy Spirit. As we intentionally focus on and become present to the inner meaning of the Scripture passage, the Holy Spirit enlightens our minds and hearts. We come to the text willing to be influenced by a deeper meaning that lies within the words and thoughts we ponder.

In this space, we open ourselves to be challenged and changed by the inner meaning we experience. We approach the text in a spirit of faith and obedience as a disciple ready to be taught by the Holy Spirit. As we savor the sacred text, we let go of our usual control of how we expect God to act in our lives and surrender our hearts and consciences to the flow of the divine (*divina*) through the reading (*lectio*).

The fundamental principle of *lectio divina* leads us to understand the profound mystery of the Incarnation, "The Word became flesh," not only in history but also within us.

## Praying *Lectio* Today

Before you begin, relax your body and maintain a posture of prayer (back straight, eyes shut, feet flat on the floor). Then practice these simple actions:

1. Read a passage from Scripture or the daily Mass readings. This is known as *lectio*. (If the Word of God is read aloud, the hearers listen attentively.)

2. Pray the selected passage with attention as you listen for a specific meaning that comes to mind. Once again, the reading is listened to or silently read and reflected or meditated on. This is known as *meditatio*.

3. The exercise becomes active. Pick a word, sentence, or idea that surfaces from your consideration of the chosen text. Does the reading remind you of a person, place, or experience? If so, pray about it. Compose your thoughts and reflection into a simple word or phrase. This prayer-thought will help you remove distractions during the *lectio*. This exercise is called *oratio*.

4. In silence, with your eyes closed, quiet yourself and become conscious of your breathing. Let your thoughts, feelings, and concerns fade as you consider the selected passage in the previous step (*oratio*). If you're distracted, use your prayer word to help you return to silence. This is *contemplatio*.

This exercise can take as long as you want, but in the context of this Bible study, 10 to 20 minutes should be sufficient.

Many teachers of prayer call contemplation the prayer of resting in God, a prelude to losing oneself in the presence of God. Scripture is transformed in our hearing as we pray and allow our hearts to unite intimately with the Lord. The Word truly takes on flesh, and this time it is manifested in our flesh.

# How to Use This Bible-Study Companion

THE BIBLE, along with the commentaries and reflections found in this study, will help participants become familiar with the Scripture texts and lead them to reflect more deeply on the texts' message. At the end of this study, participants will have a firm grasp of Isaiah, Jeremiah, Lamentations, and Baruch, becoming more cognizant of the spiritual nourishment these books offer. The reflections lead participants into their own journey with the Scripture readings.

## Context

When the authors wrote and edited the Books of Isaiah, Jeremiah, Lamentations, and Baruch, they were dealing mainly with the era of the Babylonian invasion of Judah, the exile, and the period after the exile. To help readers learn about each passage in relation to those around it, each lesson begins with an overview that puts the Scripture passages into context.

## Part 1: Group Study

To give participants a comprehensive study of the Books of Isaiah, Jeremiah, Lamentations, and Baruch, this text is divided into eight lessons. Lesson 1 is group study only; Lessons 2 through 8 are divided into Part 1, group study, and Part 2, individual study. For example, Lesson 2 covers Isaiah 6—39. The study group reads and discusses only Isaiah 6—8 (Part 1). Participants privately read and reflect on Isaiah 9—39 (Part 2).

Group study may or may not include *lectio divina*. With *lectio divina*, the group meets for ninety minutes using the format at the top of page 14. Without *lectio divina*, the group meets for one hour using the format at the bottom of page 14, and participants are urged to privately read the *lectio divina* section at the end of Part 1. It contains additional reflections on the Scripture passages studied during the group session that will take participants even further into the passages.

## Part 2: Individual Study

The Scripture passages not covered in Part 1 are divided into shorter components, one to be studied each day. Participants who don't belong to a study group can use the lessons for private sacred reading. They may choose to reflect on one Scripture passage per day, making it possible for a clearer understanding of the Scripture passages used in their *lectio divina* (sacred reading).

## A PROCESS FOR SACRED READING

Liguori Publications has designed this study to be user friendly and manageable. However, group dynamics and leaders vary. We're not trying to keep the Holy Spirit from working in your midst, thus we suggest you decide beforehand which format works best for your group. If you have limited time, you could study the Bible as a group and save prayer and reflection for personal time.

However, if your group wishes to digest and feast on sacred Scripture through both prayer and study, we recommend you spend closer to ninety minutes each week by gathering to study and pray with Scripture. *Lectio divina* (see page 9) is an ancient contemplative prayer form that moves readers from the head to the heart in meeting the Lord. We strongly suggest using this prayer form whether in individual or group study.

## GROUP-STUDY FORMATS

### 1. Bible Study With *Lectio Divina*

*About ninety minutes of group study*

- ⊞ Gathering and opening prayer (3–5 minutes)
- ⊞ Scripture passage read aloud (5 minutes)
- ⊞ Silently review the commentary and prepare to discuss it with the group (3–5 minutes)
- ⊞ Discuss the Scripture passage along with the commentary and reflection (30 minutes)
- ⊞ Scripture passage read aloud a second time, followed by quiet time for meditation and contemplation (5 minutes)
- ⊞ Spend some time in prayer with the selected passage. Group participants will slowly read the Scripture passage a third time in silence, listening for the voice of God as they read (10–20 minutes)
- ⊞ Shared reflection (10–15 minutes)
- ⊞ Closing prayer (3–5 minutes)

*To become acquainted with* lectio divina, *see page 9.*

### 2. Bible Study

*About one hour of group study*

- ⊞ Gathering and opening prayer (3–5 minutes)
- ⊞ Scripture passage read aloud (5 minutes)
- ⊞ Silently review the commentary and prepare to discuss it with the group (3–5 minutes)
- ⊞ Discuss the Scripture passage along with the commentary and reflection (40 minutes)
- ⊞ Closing prayer (3–5 minutes)

## Notes to the Leader

- ✠ Bring a copy of the *New American Bible,* revised edition.
- ✠ Plan which sections will be covered each week of your Bible study.
- ✠ Read the material in advance of each session.
- ✠ Establish written ground rules. (Example: We won't keep you longer than ninety minutes; don't dominate the sharing by arguing or debating.)
- ✠ Meet in an appropriate and welcoming gathering space (church building, meeting room, house).
- ✠ Provide name tags and perhaps use a brief icebreaker for the first meeting; ask participants to introduce themselves.
- ✠ Mark the Scripture passage(s) that will be read during the session.
- ✠ Decide how you would like the Scripture to be read aloud (whether by one or multiple readers).
- ✠ Use a clock or watch.
- ✠ Provide extra Bibles (or copies of the Scripture passages) for participants who don't bring their Bible.
- ✠ Ask participants to read "Introduction: Prophets I" (page 17) before the first session.
- ✠ Tell participants which passages to study and urge them to read the passages and commentaries before the meeting.
- ✠ If you opt to use the *lectio divina* format, familiarize yourself with this prayer form ahead of time.

## Notes to Participants

- ✠ Bring a copy of the *New American Bible,* revised edition.
- ✠ Read "Introduction: Prophets I" (page 17) before the first session.
- ✠ Read the Scripture passages and commentaries before each session.
- ✠ Be prepared to share and listen respectfully. (This is not a time to debate beliefs or argue.)

## Opening Prayer

*Leader:*     O God, come to my assistance.

*Response:* O Lord, make haste to help me.

*Leader:*     Glory be to the Father, and to the Son, and to the Holy Spirit...

*Response:* ...as it was in the beginning, is now, and ever shall be, world without end. Amen.

*Leader:*     Christ is the vine and we are the branches. As branches linked to Jesus, the vine, we are called to recognize that the Scriptures are always being fulfilled in our lives. It is the living Word of God living on in us. Come, Holy Spirit, fill the hearts of your faithful and kindle in us the fire of your divine wisdom, knowledge, and love.

*Response:* Open our minds and hearts as we study your great love for us as shown in the Bible.

*Reader:*     (Open your Bible to the assigned Scripture(s) and read in a paced, deliberate manner. Pause for one minute, listening for a word, phrase, or image that you may use in your *lectio divina* practice.)

## Closing Prayer

*Leader:*     Let us pray as Jesus taught us.

*Response:* Our Father...

*Leader:*     Lord, inspire us with your Spirit as we study your Word in the Bible. Be with us this day and every day as we strive to know you and serve you and to love as you love. We believe that through your goodness and love, the Spirit of the Lord is truly upon us. Allow the words of the Bible, your Word, to capture us and inspire us to live as you live and to love as you love.

*Response:* Amen.

*Leader:*     May divine assistance remain with us always.

*Response:* In the name of the Father, and of the Son, and of the Holy Spirit. Amen.

# Prophets I

## ISAIAH, JEREMIAH, LAMENTATIONS, BARUCH

*Read this overview before the first session.*

The role of the prophets was to communicate God's message to the people and to communicate with the Lord on behalf of the people. Prophets did not receive their office through heredity, as did the priests of the Old Testament, but they received their call from God, often through an intermediary sent by God. Since they were chosen by the Lord, prophets often began their message with the words, "Thus says the Lord," or something similar. Unlike the priesthood of the Old Testament, which was limited to males, prophets could be male or female. In the Book of Judges, a woman named Deborah is identified as a prophet (see Judges 4:4).

### Former and Latter Prophets

Among the prophets, there were some who had their words committed to writing, such as Isaiah and Jeremiah, and others who did not have their words committed to writing, such as Nathan, Elijah, and Elisha. Nathan advised King David, and Elijah and Elisha challenged the kings of the northern kingdom of Israel to remain faithful to the Lord. The historical books that described the exploits of leaders such as Moses, Joshua, the judges, Samuel, the kings, and others were considered prophetical books. The prophets included in the historical books and who did not commit their prophecies to writing are known as former prophets, while those whose names the prophetic writings bear are known as the latter prophets.

The prophets communicated these dreams or visions through oracles, discourses, or symbolic actions. Besides the prophetic teachings found in the books of the prophets, the reader also encounters narrative sections in these books that offer insights and information concerning the prophets.

## Major and Minor Prophets

Among the prophetic books, there are four major and twelve minor prophetical writings. The terms major and minor refer to the length of the writings. The major prophets include the writings of Isaiah, Jeremiah, Ezekiel, and Daniel. The minor prophets include the writings of Hosea, Joel, Amos, Obadiah, Jonah, Micah, Nahum, Habakkuk, Zephaniah, Haggai, Zechariah, and Malachi.

The Books of Lamentations and Baruch, although they are found among the prophetic books in the Catholic Bible, are not counted among the writings of the prophets in the Hebrew Bible. In the Hebrew Bible, the Book of Lamentations was one of the books found among a group known as the Writings, which also included the Book of Daniel. The Catholic Bible places the Book of Daniel among the prophetic books. The Book of Baruch is not found in the Hebrew Bible, but it is in the Greek translation of the Bible and is accepted by the Church as inspired.

Although we refer to the prophetic writings as "books," they are often a composite of the prophetic messages written or spoken by the prophet. In many cases, the followers of the prophets would hear the prophet's spoken message and later put it in writing. The writings of the prophets could also be revealed at one time in the history of Israel and, when the historical climate had changed, committed to writing or editing at a later time. Some prophetic writings were edited several times throughout history before they reached their final form.

Although many people seem to think of prophets as predicting the future, the prophets mainly addressed the current issues of their era. At times they did predict the future, often as a warning about some destruction that was to visit the people if they did not turn their hearts back to the Lord. Some also predicted a time of peace and redemption. These prophets castigated leaders who abused their power, afflicted the poor, or took advantage of the weakness of the people. They sought to persuade, encourage, and bring a future hope to the people who were suffering affliction.

The sting of the wrath of the prophets was especially felt by rulers and kings when the prophets predicted the dire consequences the Lord would afflict on those who used their power to act unjustly, or who turned to the worship of false idols. The prophets were totally dedicated to the Lord and the covenant and never failed to speak out courageously in the face of their own oppression and persecution. They addressed local, political, and international issues.

This volume of the *Liguori Catholic Bible Study* series will study the Books of Isaiah, Jeremiah, Lamentations, and Baruch.

## Historical Perspective

The history of Israel consists of four major periods that would naturally affect the manner of writing and the interpretations given to the writing by later editors.

1. The **first period** includes the era of the kings in Israel and Judah, from the eleventh to the ninth century before Christ.

2. The **second period** includes the era of Assyrian domination, which took place in the eighth century when Assyria conquered the northern kingdom of Israel in 721 BC, sending many of its inhabitants into exile.

3. The **third period** includes the Babylonian crisis that took place from the seventh century to the early part of the sixth century before Christ, when Babylon invaded Judah and led many of its inhabitants into exile.

4. The **fourth period** includes the era from the late sixth to the middle of the fifth century before Christ, when Cyrus of Persia conquered the Babylonians and allowed the Israelites to return home to Judah.

## LESSON 1

# The Book of Isaiah (I)

### ISAIAH 1–5

*In days to come, the mountain of the LORD's house shall be established as the highest mountain and raised above the hills. All nations shall stream toward it. Many peoples shall come and say: "Come, let us go up to the LORD's mountain, to the house of the God of Jacob" (2:2–3).*

**Opening Prayer** (SEE PAGE 16)

### Context

**The Book of Isaiah 1:1—5:30** Scripture scholars note three separate divisions in the Book of Isaiah, written by at least three different authors at three different periods in history. They identify the divisions as First Isaiah (1—39), Second Isaiah (40—55), and Third Isaiah (56—66). Since the total Book of Isaiah includes a number of authors and editors living during the three centuries after First Isaiah, later editors were able to add to and interpret portions of earlier Isaiah according to their own social, political, and historical situations. Because they placed this material wherever they wished in the text, the material in the Book of Isaiah does not always follow a chronological order. For example, Isaiah received his call to become a prophet in chapter 6 after acting as a prophet in the first five chapters.

The first five chapters of the Book of Isaiah found in Part 1 of this study present an occurring theme found throughout the book. The Lord (1) warns the people of the punishment in store if they refuse to worship the true God of the Israelites, (2) relents and promises the restoration of Zion, and (3) punishes those who worship false gods or unjustly treat others.

## GROUP STUDY (ISAIAH 1—5)

Read aloud Isaiah 1—5.

### 1:1–31 Accusation and Purification

The writing begins with Isaiah's declaration that he had a vision. Since the vision is mentioned at the beginning of the book, it implies that the remainder of the writing results from the vision. The writer identifies himself as Isaiah, a name that means "the salvation of the Lord."

The vision concerns Judah and Jerusalem. After the death of Solomon, inhabitants of the northern kingdom of Israel rebelled against Solomon's son and formed their own kingdom composed of ten of the tribes of Israel, which became known as the kingdom of Israel. Solomon's son retained control over two of the tribes of Israel, which were the tribes of Judah and Benjamin (see 1 Kings 21). The southern kingdom became known as the kingdom of Judah. Isaiah dates his era by naming the kings of Judah, from King Uzziah to the reign of King Hezekiah, which would place his ministry as lasting from 742 BC to 701 BC, or even longer until the death of Hezekiah in 687 BC.

During his lifetime, Isaiah uttered many oracles, which his followers recalled and eventually put in writing. In these oracles, the Lord refers to the people of Israel as the Lord's sons and daughters. Unfortunately, because they rebelled against the Lord, the Lord threatened to destroy them with death (see Deuteronomy 32). Unlike the dumb ox and ass who know their master, Isaiah says the Lord's own people do not recognize their true master, the Lord.

The Lord refers to Israel as sinful, wicked, corrupt children who have rebelled against the Lord, the Holy One of Israel. This theme will occur often in the writings of Isaiah. The title "Holy One of Israel" will appear throughout the book when speaking of the Lord.

Around the year 701 BC, when Isaiah was prophesying, the powerful Assyrian army was inflicting heavy casualties on the people of Judah. The prophet speaks of strangers, a reference to the Assyrians, who ravaged and burned the land to the point it became a wasteland like Sodom, which the Lord destroyed with fire (see Genesis 19 for the story of Sodom and Gomorrah). The prophet refers to Jerusalem as daughter Zion and compares her to a hut in a vineyard. The once glorious and powerful city has become like a tiny shelter for laborers in a vineyard or a melon field. This hut points to the remnant of the people who will save the Israelites from the type of total destruction afflicted on the people of Sodom and Gomorrah.

The Lord decries the hypocrisy of the people, who remain faithful to the externals of worship but who caused pain for the poor. The Lord seeks justice for the people, especially by helping orphans and widows. Although the people have sinned gravely, the Lord tells them that if they repent, their sins will become as white as snow or wool. The people will share in the good things of the world if they are faithful and obedient to the Lord, or they will be destroyed by the sword if they resist the Lord's call to repentance.

The Lord bemoans Judah's abandonment of the worship of the one true God when they chose instead to worship idols. The Scriptures often refer to those who break the covenant and worship false gods as prostitutes. Jerusalem, which was so faithful and concerned for justice, has now become depraved. Those who once helped the people now look for bribes and gifts for themselves, while neglecting to help orphans and widows. The fierce judgment of the Lord will come upon them and the Lord will seek revenge on those who act without justice. The hope Isaiah offered is that eventually Jerusalem will again be a city of justice and righteousness, and the rebellious and sinners will be destroyed.

### 2:1–22 Peace and Destruction

In another vision, Isaiah speaks of the glory of the Lord that is to come. He writes the highest mountain shall be the mountain of the Lord's house. He is not speaking in human terms but in spiritual terms. The Lord's house refers to the Temple, and the highest mountain refers to Jerusalem, which is obviously not the highest material mountain, as the author claims. The passage views Jerusalem as perched above the world, seeing and being seen by all. Nations shall stream toward this mountain, and people shall climb this mountain to the Lord's house, which means they will choose to worship the Lord of Israel, the God of Jacob, in the Temple.

Since Zion knows the Lord, instruction in the ways of the Lord shall come forth from the people of Jerusalem to other nations. The message from the mountain of the Lord shall be a message of peace, a time when people will make implements of war, such as swords and spears, into implements for gardening (plowshares and pruning hooks). Wars will cease. Once people accept the God of Israel as Lord over all, they will come before the Lord on the holy mountain to settle their disputes in peace rather than in war.

The mood changes from peace before the Lord to the Lord's judgment on the people. It is the Day of the Lord. The Lord accuses the Israelites (house of Jacob) of abandoning the people. The Lord tells Isaiah the land is filled with the false worship of gods, diviners, and soothsayers, and like the foreign Philistines who also inhabit the land, they join hands with all foreigners for the sake of commercial gain. They possess silver, gold, horses, and chariots and fill the land with idols and images made by humans. The day of the Lord is a day when sinners should hide themselves from the Lord behind rocks and in the dust, as though the Lord will not find them.

On that day, the Lord will be recognized as the exalted one, humbling the proud and arrogant, and bringing low those who hold themselves in high esteem. All the wealth and power leading people to act with arrogant pride will no longer matter. The mighty cedars of Lebanon and the oaks of Bashan shall be brought low. These impressive trees were held in high esteem for building.

On the day of the Lord, the people will rid themselves of their idols, no matter how valuable and ornate, throwing them to the unclean moles and bats.

### 3:1—4:6 Judgments Against Jerusalem and Judah

This passage speaks of devastation in Jerusalem and Judah, an apparent reference to the time when the Assyrians ravaged Judah around the year

701 BC. On the day the enemy conquers the nation, they will take away the leading people of the land whom Isaiah names as the heroes, warriors, judges, prophets, elders, captains, nobles, and the skilled workers. The Lord will leave them in a situation where no one will want to lead them. Chaos and anarchy will dominate. The people will seek leaders who protest that they themselves are weak and in need.

Isaiah tells the people the Lord will bless those who are just, enabling them to prosper and eat the food they produce. Since invading armies confiscated all the produce from the land, eating the food the people produce was a way of telling the people they would not be invaded. On the other hand, those who are evil will experience evil in return. The chaos will become so drastic that infants will be the ones to oppress the people. Some commentators believe this is a reference to Ahaz, who apparently became king at a young age. The Lord will pass a dire judgment on those who oppressed the poor and weak, consumed their vineyards, and looted their homes.

The judgment of the Lord challenges the haughtiness and adornments of the women, a reference to women of wealth. The day will come when the Lord will afflict them with repugnant scabs on their shaven heads. Laying bare a woman's head by shaving her hair is a sign of public shame. In place of their perfume will be a stench, instead of a sash will be a common rope, instead of hair will be baldness, instead of a precious gown will be sackcloth, and instead of beauty will be shame.

In Israelite society, a woman who did not give birth to a child was disgraced. With the slaughter of so many men during the Assyrian invasion, a group of women will seek to have a child from the same man, not competing with each other, but receiving food and clothing if he will give them his name, that is, marry them and have a child with them. In the Book of Exodus, the Lord, speaking to Moses, commands a man who takes more than one wife to provide food and clothing for each wife (see Exodus 21:10).

The Lord speaks to Isaiah about a day of blessing. It will be a day when the branch of the Lord will be beautiful and glorious and the fruit of the land will bring pride and glory to the survivors of Israel. The imagery of a branch of the Lord often refers to the Davidic kingship, but in this case it refers to the community of Israel. The survivors left in Zion, Jerusalem, will be called holy and inscribed for life in Jerusalem.

When the Lord brings about this new cleansing from the filth of the daughters of Zion and purges Jerusalem's blood from their midst, the glory of the Lord will be with Zion again. The filth of the daughters of Zion may refer to the menstrual blood of women that Mosaic Law saw as needing a ritual cleansing. In this passage, the Lord provides a ritual cleansing for Zion. The smoking cloud by day and the light of a flaming fire by night will be the glory of the Lord sheltering the people from the elements. The image of the smoking cloud by day and the flaming fire by night recalls the passage in Exodus where the Lord preceded the people of Israel in the desert as a column of cloud by day and a column of fire by night (see Exodus 13:21–22).

### 5:1–30 The Song of the Vineyard

Isaiah presents his message with a poetic story, telling how his beloved friend established a vineyard on a fertile hillside. The friend is a reference to the Lord and the vineyard a reference to Israel. In Psalm 80, we read: "You brought a vine out of Egypt; you drove out nations and planted it" (Psalm 80:9). Like a farmer, the Lord prepared the vineyard (the Promised Land), digging it up, clearing it, and planting the vines, making it a flourishing vineyard.

In ancient times, a watchtower was often placed in the vineyard and a hedge built around it to protect it from vandalism or theft. The people of Israel built their watchtowers right into the walls around their cities. The Lord prepared a winepress for the vineyard, a sign that the vineyard (the people) would produce sweet grapes. Instead of producing a crop of good grapes, the Israelites produced rotten grapes. That is, they sinned.

When the people of Israel break their part of the covenant with the Lord, the Lord will take away the vineyard's hedge (the walls of the city), allowing it to be infested with thorns, briers, and wild animals and letting other nations trample over it. The Lord will withhold the rain and the vineyard will end up desolate, waterless, and empty.

Isaiah receives news about the woes cast upon the rich people of Israel by the Lord. These woes will take place when the Assyrians later invade

Israel and reduce the wealthy to a punishment of exile or poverty. The woes are expressed by the word "Ah."

The first woe condemns those who confiscate homes and land from the poor, connecting house to house and field to field until they leave nothing for the poor. They will be punished. Ten acres of a vineyard shall yield one bath (about twelve gallons) of wine. A homer of seed, which would ordinarily yield ten bushels of wheat, will yield only one bushel.

The second woe refers to those who overindulge in drink and revelry, celebrating with musical instruments while ignoring the Lord. As a punishment for not appreciating all the Lord has done for them, they will go into exile. The Lord's judgment becomes visible when the lambs and goats graze freely in the ruins left behind by the rich.

The third woe concerns those who drag sin along with them as though they are tugging a stubborn animal. They carry guilt with them, scoffing at the predictions given by Isaiah concerning the destruction in store for them. They sarcastically call on the Holy One (the Lord) to hurry and fulfill this dire prediction so that they can believe it.

The fourth woe concerns those who refuse to acknowledge their evil ways. For them, evil is good and good is evil, darkness is light and light is darkness. They profit from evil and avoid goodness.

The fifth woe is cast on those who are wise and prudent in their own eyes. Their wisdom is their own, not the wisdom of the Lord.

The sixth woe falls on those who are corrupt. Isaiah is pointing out the wickedness of the leaders and the rich nobles, who indulge themselves with alcohol while accepting bribes to announce judgments of innocence for the guilty. They deprive the innocent of justice. Because of their sins, they shall shrivel like dry grass, and like dry blossoms they will be scattered around like dust.

The Lord will summon men from a nation from far away who will come speedily with great agility and energy, well-armored for battle, with bows and arrows ready, and riding in chariots drawn by swift horses. Like lions, they will pounce on the helpless people of Judah. Darkness is closing in on Judah, a reference to reading the signs of the times that indicate the Assyrians are about to ravage the land.

## *Review Questions*

1. Why does the Lord reject the offering of the people?
2. What does the author mean when he says Jerusalem has become a prostitute?
3. Why does the Lord cast an unfavorable judgment on Jerusalem?
4. What is the message of the song of the vineyard?

---

**Closing Prayer** (SEE PAGE 16)

Pray the closing prayer now or after *lectio divina*.

---

### *Lectio Divina* (SEE PAGE 9)

Relax your body and maintain a posture of prayer (back straight, eyes shut, feet flat on the floor). This exercise can take as long as you want, but in the context of this Bible study, 10 to 20 minutes should be sufficient.

The meditations that follow are provided only to help group participants use this prayer form, but note that *lectio* is intended to bring one to a place of prayerful contemplation where the Word of God speaks to the hearer from his or her heart. (See page 9 for further instruction.)

### *Accusation and Purification (1:1–31)*

An article in a newspaper related how a man, who sold mortgages with fees hidden from unsuspecting buyers, forced people into foreclosure. He never viewed himself as being a bad person, just a shrewd businessman. He even worshiped with his community every Sunday. In many ways, he could be like the people of Judah in the time of Isaiah. They could harm the orphan and widow and still come before the Lord to offer their sacrifices. The Lord had to reject their offerings because they lacked the true spirit of worship, namely concern for others.

We are not to judge the spiritual motives of the businessman who brought pain into the lives of others, but we are to examine our own life. Do we have a spirit of love and concern for our neighbors?

✠ *What can I learn from this passage?*

### *Peace and Destruction (2:1–22)*

An ideal life would be one where there is love for each other, where no one dislikes us, we trust our neighbor, and everyone shares with one another. It is a life where people will beat their swords into plowshares and their spears into pruning hooks. We know we will not find such a world here, but the Lord seems to believe we can strive in that direction.

✠ *What can I learn from this passage?*

### *Judgments Against Jerusalem and Judah (3:1—4:6)*

A woman worried about her son who, for the first time, left home to attend college. She told a friend a time comes when parents have to let their children live their own lives, as difficult as it may be. God does the same. In giving us free will, God is saying it's time for us to be on our own. The Lord could have saved the people of Israel and Judah from their own missteps and sins, but God had to let them go and experience the joys or pain that come with loving or not loving the Lord. The Lord will always be with us, leading us as the Lord led the Israelites, but the Lord will always allow us to choose to remain faithful or not remain faithful to our commitment to the Lord.

✠ *What can I learn from this passage?*

### *The Song of the Vineyard (5:1–30)*

The image of the friend who has a vineyard recalls the words of Jesus, who depicts himself as a vine and his followers as the branches. Unlike the Israelites, who center the fulfillment of God's promise on the gift of the Promised Land as the Lord's vineyard, Christians view the fulfillment of God's promise in a person, namely Jesus, whose presence fills the whole world. In the New Testament, Jesus is the vine and we are the branches (see John 15:5). Wherever we are in the world, we have the call to remain faithful to Christ so our lives may bear good fruit. The good we do in the world comes from the vine, Jesus Christ.

✠ *What can I learn from this passage?*

---

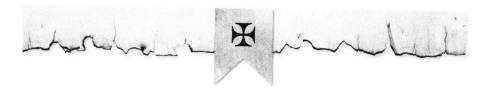

# The Book of Isaiah (II)

### ISAIAH 6—39

*The people who walked in darkness have seen a great light;*
*Upon those who lived in a land of gloom a light has shone (9:1).*

## Opening Prayer (SEE PAGE 16)

## Context

**Part 1: Isaiah 6—9:6** The Lord calls Isaiah for his mission as a prophet. As part of his mission, Isaiah attempts to convince Ahaz not to align himself with the Assyrians against the threatening invasion of the northern kingdom (Ephraim).

**Part 2: Isaiah 9:7—39:8** The Lord promises to provide salvation under a new, ideal king of the line of David, leading to a restoration in Judah. Isaiah speaks of the Lord's threat of destruction for Assyria and lists oracles of destruction against the nations. The Lord warns against Judah joining an alliance with Egypt to fight against the Assyrians and predicts the total destruction will come from Babylon.

## PART 1: GROUP STUDY (ISAIAH 6—9:6)

Read aloud Isaiah 6—9:6.

### 6:1–13 Isaiah's Mission

In the year King Uzziah died (about 742 BC), Isaiah received his call to serve the Lord. He saw the Lord seated on a towering throne in a Temple, clothed in garments filling the Temple. In his vision, he sees Seraphim that resemble the image found in the Holy of Holies in the Jerusalem Temple. They have six large wings, with two covering their faces, two covering their feet, and two that allowed them to hover over the assembly. They are messengers of the Lord.

One of the Seraphim proclaims the Lord, whose glory fills the earth, is holy. The glory of the Lord becomes visible with the shaking of the door frame and smoke filling the Temple. The scene recalls a passage from Exodus when a cloud covered the meeting tent, which was the tent where the Lord dwelt with the Israelites during their journey through the desert. The cloud indicated the glory of the Lord filled the tent (see Exodus 40:34).

Isaiah recognizes his human condition as something lowly, calling himself a person of unclean lips living among people of unclean lips. One of the Seraphim takes an ember with a tong from the altar and touches Isaiah's lips, declaring that his wickedness has been cleansed. Isaiah hears the Lord ask, "Whom shall I send" (6:8), and Isaiah responds that the Lord should send him.

In response, the Lord sends Isaiah on his mission. He instructs him to inform the people that they will listen but not understand. If they were faithful, they would experience healing. Since living faithfully means trusting the Lord rather than trusting the armies of other countries, the people reject Isaiah's prophecies, refusing to trust the power of the Lord.

In frustration, Isaiah asks the Lord how much time these people will be given before they realize their need to trust the Lord. The Lord responds the people will experience desolation, vacant cities, and houses, and exile to a far-away land. Even the smallest remnant shall be destroyed, like a tree whose trunk remains when its leaves have fallen. A hint of hope for the future comes when the Lord states that the trunk will remain. A new generation will sprout from this trunk.

### 7:1–25 Emmanuel

Isaiah had a special mission during the reign of Ahaz, the king of Judah who reigned from 735 to 715 BC. When the Assyrians became a powerful nation and threatened to invade the northern kingdom and its ally, Syria, the kings of both kingdoms tried to convince Ahaz, the king of Judah, to join them against the Assyrians. Ahaz refused and, as a result, the two kings attacked the kingdom of Judah with the hope of replacing Ahaz with a king who would join them in their war against the Assyrians. The war with Syria and the northern kingdom became known as the Syro-Ephraimite War. Isaiah often referred to the northern kingdom of Israel by the name of Ephraim, the most important tribe of the northern kingdom.

The Lord sends Isaiah to deliver an oracle to Ahaz. Isaiah's son, Shear-jashub, travels with him. The son's name points to the future, since it means "a remnant will return." Isaiah predicts the kingdoms of Aram and Ephraim will not survive.

Isaiah instructs Ahaz to ask for a sign that Judah will not be totally destroyed, but Ahaz refuses, saying he will not tempt the Lord. Although Ahaz refuses to seek a sign, Isaiah gives him one, stating that a young woman will give birth to a son who will be called "Emmanuel." This prediction in the Hebrew text points to a son for Ahaz, a sign that the Davidic line would not end with Ahaz. The child to be born of the young woman shall eat curds and honey, which will be the only food available left for those who remain in the ravaged land.

The Septuagint translation changed the term "a young woman" to "a virgin." Although it refers to a son for Ahaz, Christian writers, taking their cue from the Gospel of Matthew, view it as a prediction pointing to Mary and the birth of Jesus (see Matthew 1:22–23).

The king of Assyria captures and destroys the northern kingdom, and later plunders the cities of Judah. Because Ahaz asked Assyria for help against Syria and the northern kingdom, Isaiah predicted the devastation of the land of Judah will be worse than the time the northern kingdom

(Ephraim) cut itself off from Judah (see 1 Kings 12). Egypt and Assyria, pictured as insects, will appear and cover the land like flies and bees.

The land of Judah shall experience total devastation. The survivors will live poorly, keeping a young cow and a couple of sheep and eating curds from their yield of milk. Briars and thorns will cover the vines that once enriched the people.

### 8:1–22 Light and Darkness

Isaiah marries a prophetess who bore a son named Maher-shalal-hash-baz. The name means "quick spoils, speedy plunder." The Lord predicts that before the child is old enough to speak, the Assyrians will have plundered the northern kingdom.

Isaiah delivers another oracle from the Lord. A gentle stream of water, known as the waters of Shiloah, provided drink for the people of Judah during a siege. Rejecting the Lord is symbolized by rejecting the waters of Shiloah. Because the people rejected the gentle providence of the Lord, the Lord will overwhelm them with the waters of the "River," which refers to the Euphrates and in this case symbolically refers to the Assyrians. The Assyrian invasion will inundate Judah.

The Lord again offers some hope to the people. The Assyrians, a people from a distant land, shall eventually be defeated. Because the Lord is with the people of Judah, they will not be able to capture the land as they did the northern kingdom.

Because Isaiah and his followers oppose joining with the Assyrians, they are considered conspirators. The Lord directs them not to fear the people but to trust the Lord, who is the one to fear. In disobeying the Lord, both Judah and Syria will fall into a trap.

Isaiah sounds a warning against those who call upon the dead as though they were gods, predicting they will find only darkness without the dawning of light. They will live in a land where they are hungry, and when hungry, they will lose hope and become enraged against their kings and their gods.

### 8:23—9:6 Salvation Under a New Davidic King

The land of Zebulun and Naphtali, part of the northern kingdom, experienced the ravages of the Assyrian invasion. The way of the sea is the area along the Mediterranean that became an Assyrian province. These once-devastated areas will see a great light. The Lord will bring them a reason for joy with a generous harvest and freedom from the yoke of the Assyrians that burdened them. Their oppressors will be smashed, as on the day of Midian. Midian was the place where Gideon led 300 Israelites against a strong Midian army and, with the help of the Lord, claimed an unlikely victory (see Judges 6—7).

Isaiah declares that a son is born for us and dominion rests on his shoulders, an image that appears to be borrowed from the inauguration of a new ruler. This new ruler seems to be Hezekiah, the son of Ahaz, for whom Isaiah has great hopes and who seems to be the Emmanuel mentioned earlier. "They name him Wonder-Counselor, God-Hero, Father-Forever, Prince of Peace" (9:5). By naming him Father-Forever, the prophet does not declare that he will live forever but that he will always act fatherly.

## Review Questions

1. What are some significant points in Isaiah's call to mission?
2. What does Isaiah mean when he speaks of a child who shall be named "Emmanuel?"
3. Who is the child Isaiah is speaking about when he says that a child is born for us?

---

### Closing Prayer (SEE PAGE 16)

Pray the closing prayer now or after *lectio divina*.

---

### Lectio Divina (SEE PAGE 9)

Relax your body and maintain a posture of prayer (back straight, eyes shut, feet flat on the floor). This exercise can take as long as you want, but in the context of this Bible study, 10 to 20 minutes should be sufficient.

The meditations that follow are provided only to help group participants use this prayer form, but note that *lectio* is intended to bring one to a place of prayerful contemplation where the Word of God speaks to the hearer from his or her heart. (See page 9 for further instruction.)

### Isaiah's Mission (6:1–13)

Jesus told his disciples, "You have not chosen me, I have chosen you." Just as the Lord sent Isaiah on his mission, so the Lord gives each one of us a mission. In the Sacrament of Baptism, Jesus touched our hearts with the burning coal of his love and power, giving us a special mission of making Christ visible in the world through our manner of life.

✠ *What can I learn from this passage?*

### Emmanuel (7:1–25)

Near the beginning of the Gospel of Matthew, we read, "Behold, the virgin shall be with child and bear a son, and they shall name him Emmanuel, which means 'God is with us'" (Matthew 1:23). At the end of Matthew's Gospel, we read, "And behold, I am with you always, until the end of the age" (Matthew 28:20). Just as the Lord was with the line of David in the time of Ahaz, the Lord is present with us today. Jesus, Emmanuel, promised to be with us until the end of time.

✠ *What can I learn from this passage?*

### Light and Darkness (8:1–22)

In speaking to a woman at a well, Jesus says "whoever drinks the water I shall give will never thirst" (John 4:14). When Jesus uses this image of water, he is not speaking about physical thirst but a thirst for God's presence in our lives. In the same way, when Isaiah speaks of the gentle waters of Shiloah, he is speaking of the blessings and protection of the Lord. The message is that the Lord provides for our needs and brings fulfillment to our lives, but we must trust the Lord and remain faithful.

✠ *What can I learn from this passage?*

### Salvation Under a New Davidic King (8:23—9:6)

In Matthew's Gospel, we read Jesus went to live in Capernaum by the Sea, in the region of Zebulun and Naphtali, as a fulfillment of the prophecy of Isaiah who declared the land of Zebulun and land of Naphtali have seen a great light. Jesus, the Light of the World, chose to live in this area during his public mission. In our life, Jesus fills us with the light of his presence, helping us to endure our darkest moments.

✠ *What can I learn from this passage?*

## PART 2: INDIVIDUAL STUDY (ISAIAH 9:7—39:8)

### Day 1: The Arrogant Assyrians and the Salvation of Israel (9:7—12:6)

The Lord sends word to the northern kingdom, often referred to under the names of Israel, Ephraim, or those who dwell in Samaria. They brag they have endured destruction but will survive, using the images of fallen bricks that will be replaced with cut stone or cut-down sycamore trees that will be replaced by cedars.

The people, however, refuse to turn back to the Lord, so the Lord cuts off their heads (the elders and the nobles) and their tails (the false prophets). Manasseh devours Ephraim and likewise Ephraim devours Manasseh. Both these tribes belong to the northern kingdom. The reference implies a civil war within the kingdom with one tribe warring against another.

Isaiah speaks of a woe cast upon those who promulgate unjust decrees, depriving the needy of just judgments. After all their evil acts, they can ask themselves where they can flee for help at the time of the Assyrian invasion and to whom will they leave their wealth.

The Lord used the Assyrians as a punishing rod for the Israelites, supporting them as they plundered, looted, and trampled into the mud those who provoked the Lord's wrath. Isaiah names the cities conquered by the Assyrians. The Lord declares punishment shall come upon Jerusalem just as it came upon all idolatrous kingdoms that had more idols than those found in Jerusalem.

Because the Assyrians eventually became arrogant and proud, believing that their own power and wisdom brought about the devastation of the Israelites, the Lord abandoned them. They boast they had taken the nations as easily as a person takes eggs left in a nest with no protection. The Lord marvels at the foolishness of the Assyrians who do not recognize they are instruments of the Lord. Using rhetorical questions, the Lord asks if the ax, saw, rod, or staff can boast of its work without realizing it is the one who uses it who brings results. In a single day, the Lord, the Holy One who is the Light of Israel, will become a flame burning and consuming the wicked. The glory of the Assyrians will be consumed with a plague that will leave them wasting away.

Justice demands the destruction of many of the Israelites who had turned against the Lord. Although the Israelites had become a nation as numerous as the sands, only a remnant will remain to return home. The Lord's anger against Zion, however, is about to cease, and when it does, the Lord will destroy the Assyrians. On that day, the burden of the Assyrians will cease and the yoke around the neck of the Israelites will be shattered. From the stump of the tree of Jesse, the father of David, a shoot shall sprout and blossom. The Spirit of the Lord will come upon the offspring of Jesse, a spirit of wisdom, understanding, counsel, strength, knowledge, and fear of the Lord.

The Lord declares the that new Davidic leader will judge justly, not by appearance or by what he hears. He will deal fairly with the poor and afflicted. He will judge harshly with the ruthless and wicked. Isaiah paints a picture of ideal peace under this new Davidic king. The wild animals will live peacefully with their natural quarry, and those that eat meat will eat only vegetation. The wolf and lamb, the leopard and young goat, the calf and the young lion, the cow and the bear and their offspring, and a little child in an adder's lair shall all live together in peace. The lion will eat hay like the ox.

The Lord will reclaim a remnant of the people from Assyria, Egypt, and other areas of the four corners of the earth where the dispersed of Judah were living. The envy and hostility of Ephraim toward Judah shall cease, and Judah and Ephraim shall join ranks and plunder the Philistines of the west and the people of the east in the Arabian Desert. They shall conquer Edom, Moab, and the Ammonites, places and oppressive people their ancestors encountered in the wilderness. Isaiah speaks of the Lord drying up the tongue of the sea, which appears to be an image of the sea crossed by the Israelites when they escaped from Egypt under the leadership of Moses. The Lord will cause a great wind to form small streams out of the Euphrates River, so the dispersed can return from captivity in Assyria.

Isaiah tells the people on the day of their deliverance they will proclaim God is their salvation, filling them with confidence and courage. The city of Zion will exalt with joyful praise of the Holy One of Israel.

### Lectio Divina

Spend 8 to 10 minutes in silent contemplation of the following passage:

Despite the sinfulness of the Israelites, the Lord quickly relents when they show some slight turning back to the covenant. Jesus expresses a similar compassionate concern for the people of Jerusalem when he laments, "Jerusalem, Jerusalem, you who kill the prophets and stone those sent to you, how many times I yearned to gather your children together as a hen gathers her brood under her wings, but you were unwilling! Behold, your house will be abandoned" (Luke 13:34–35). The Lord longs to help us, the new Jerusalem, but we must respond by remaining faithful to the Lord.

✠ *What can I learn from this passage?*

## Day 2: Oracles Against Foreign Nations (13—23)

Chapters 13 through 23 contain nine oracles against foreign nations, among them Babylon. Since the power of Babylon had not reached its peak during the era of First Isaiah, portions of the chapters appear to come from a later time by a different author.

The first oracle in chapter 13 concerns Babylon. The oracle begins with the Lord calling the armies to enter the gates of the nobles, which refers to the gates of Babylon. This will take place on the day of the Lord, which usually signified the image of the Lord coming in power to destroy the enemy. The day of the Lord, besides destroying the land and sinners, will also be a time of cosmic disturbance. The stars, the sun, and the moon will not send out their light. Many people will be slaughtered, with human beings becoming rarer than the gold of Ophir. Ophir was noted for its abundance of gold.

On that day, people will flee from their homes like hunted gazelles or a runaway flock. Those who do not escape will be abused and killed. The Lord identifies the attackers as Medes. The Medes joined with Cyrus of

Persia in defeating the Babylonians. The Medes think nothing of gold or silver, which means they cannot be bribed. The author predicts glorious Babylon will be destroyed like Sodom and Gomorrah.

Chapter 14 describes the return of the people of Judah and Israel to their own land. The Lord states Sheol, the place of the dead, is preparing for the arrival of the Babylonians. All luxury and pomp of the Babylonians go down to Sheol with them, and their couch becomes a couch crawling with maggots and worms. The "Morning Star" will fall from the heavens. The Morning Star refers to the king of Babylon, although the Latin Vulgate translated the phrase as Lucifer, a name applied to Satan by early Church scholars. When the king of Babylon dies, he will become carrion, a trampled corpse with his name removed from the earth by the massacre of his sons and daughters.

In the year King Ahaz died, an oracle came from the Lord against Philistia, urging the nation not to rejoice over the death of the rod that struck them, a reference to the death of the king of Assyria. The Lord warns that another king will arise in Assyria. The Philistines will see the Assyrians coming, their horses raising the dust like smoke from the north.

Chapters 15 and 16 speak of an oracle on Moab. The Moabites suffered several natural disasters and invasions. Because of these tragedies, the people of Moab went into mourning, which involved the shaving of one's head and beard, wearing sackcloth, and sobbing—all done in public. When many of the outcasts of Moab fled like flushed-out birds seeking asylum in Zion, the Lord directed the Israelites to allow them to live among them. The Lord knew of the pride and arrogance of Moab, and now Moab must weep in humility and disgrace. All in their land is lost, including the fruits, the harvest, and the joy of the winepresses. The Lord moans for Moab, who prays to deaf idols that can do nothing.

The oracle in chapter 17 states that Damascus will become a pile of ruins and its cities abandoned. Damascus is the capital of Aram, known also as Syria. The poor of the land will seek the gleanings left over after the harvesting, but they will find very little. Because of their need, the people will turn to the Lord, the God of Israel, and not to their false gods. A later addition says the people planted for the "pleasant one," a reference to a false god. Since this addition seems out of place in the oracles, it can cause confusion for the reader.

The next oracle, found in chapter 18, concerns Ethiopia. Due to additions made at a later date, this oracle is difficult to understand. Ethiopia is addressed as the land of buzzing insects, which could refer to the land north of the Nile where there are many insects. The Egyptians sent ambassadors to Ethiopia, whose inhabitants are tall, bronzed, and feared, with the hope the Ethiopians will join them in a battle against the Assyrians.

Chapter 19 presents an oracle on Egypt. The Lord predicts a situation where Egyptians will fight Egyptians; this civil war will take place before Egypt is united. Isaiah states the Lord will bring Egypt under a cruel master, an apparent reference to the king of Assyria. Isaiah speaks about the foolishness of the princes and counselors in Egypt. A later addition to this chapter speaks about the Egyptians being like trembling women because of their fear of the Lord and Judah.

In Egypt there shall be an altar that witnesses to the Lord of hosts in Egypt, enabling the Lord to help the Egyptians when they cry out. Although the Lord punishes Egypt, the Lord will heal them when they turn to the Lord God.

Chapter 20 is a warning against trusting Egypt. Isaiah received a message not to join forces with Egypt and Ethiopia against the Assyrians. The Lord directed Isaiah to walk naked and barefoot, which he did for three years. His nakedness was meant to warn King Hezekiah this is what will happen to him and the people of Judah if he joined forces against the Assyrians. Hezekiah listened to Isaiah's warning and did not join in the rebellion. After a later battle, the general of the king of Assyria forced the captives of the Egyptians and Ethiopians to walk into captivity naked.

Chapter 21 appears to refer to a date immediately before or after the fall of Babylon, which took place in 539 BC. Two nations, Elam and Media, join with Cyrus and march under his leadership to conquer the Babylonians. Isaiah tells the nations to oil their shields in preparation for battle. When warriors went into battle, they would oil and grease their shields to deflect enemy weapons and to protect the shields. When the Babylonians are defeated, a watchman catches sight of a chariot pulled by two horses and a rider shouting out the news Babylon has fallen and all its gods smashed.

An oracle on Dumah, an oasis in Arabia, follows. Someone asks the watchman how much longer the night will be. The people of Isaiah's era referred to suffering as night. The watchman says morning has come and again night. This seems to mean suffering will come, relief will follow, and suffering will come again.

An oracle in the steppe refers to an oasis in northern Arabia with enough water to help the fugitives who are fleeing from battle. The Lord uses the phrase, "In another year, like the years of a hired laborer..." (21:16), a phrase used to designate a fixed period of time. At that time, the glory of Kadar will come to an end. The people of Kadar were expert archers who once confronted Judah.

Chapter 22 tells of an oracle on the Valley of Vision, which is west of Jerusalem. The Lord is angry, saddened over the actions of the people of Jerusalem. Their soldiers fled but were captured far from the city. There is great dread and the people call for help from other nations. They seek weapons from the House of the Forest, a building established by Solomon for storing weapons and to prepare the city for battle. They planned on a water supply and made the walls of the city firmer. They, however, neglected to look to the Lord, the city's Maker, for help. The Lord expected to find the people weeping and in mourning, but instead they celebrated, expecting to die the next day.

The Lord sends Isaiah to a man named Shebna, who was a master of the palace and who built a glorious tomb for himself that would not be used for him when he died. When he dies, the Lord appoints Eliakim as the new master of the palace. He will be like a peg in a firm place and receive all the glory of his office. Eliakim, however, sins and loses his position.

In chapter 23, an oracle about Tyre concerns the destruction of Tyre and Sidon by the Assyrians around 701 BC. Tyre became wealthy as a port for merchants. The sailors on the ships of Tarshish wail as they near the port and realize the city has been destroyed. The merchants of Sidon, who once ruled because of their wealth, will be gone. Since the people of Tyre traded with Egypt, the destruction of the merchants will cause distress for that nation. Tyre was called the one who bestowed crowns, since the merchants were so powerful that they could make and depose kings in several ports, but they will have no harbor and remain at home. In time, Tyre will return to its trading, but the trade shall be for the people of Judah.

## *Lectio Divina*

Spend 8 to 10 minutes in silent contemplation of the following passage:

> There are indeed tragedies such as those faced by the sailors of Tarshish, but there are also the normal difficulties of life that some view as terrible "woes." We will have toothaches, colds, time pressures, disagreements, rejections, misunderstandings, and a number of other minor setbacks in life. Some react to them as major "woes," while others can accept them as part of the flow of everyday life. Keeping God in the picture can help us through some very difficult "woes."

✠ *What can I learn from this passage?*

---

## Day 3: Apocalypse of Isaiah (24—27)

The following chapters, similar to many of the chapters in the Book of Isaiah, have a long history of development with additions and interpretations being added by later editors.

In chapter 24, Isaiah speaks of the Lord making the earth a wasteland, scattering all the inhabitants. Everyone will experience this devastation. The people will be punished for their sins against the ancient covenant, which some commentators believe is the covenant God made with Noah. Noah planted grape vines after the flood. Only a few inhabitants will remain on the earth, and all wine drinking and singing will end. The small number of the saved will sing for joy and praise the Lord from all ends of the earth, crying out, "Splendor to the Just One!" (24:16).

The tone changes as Isaiah, speaking on his own behalf, sees devastation all around him with the earth shaken apart because of the rebellion of the people. Those who fall into a pit will climb out only to be caught in a trap. In other words, there is no escape. The Lord will punish the hosts of heaven, a reference to the stars that the pagans revered as gods. They will be shut up in a dungeon where they will perish. Then the Lord will reign in glory on Mount Zion and in Jerusalem.

In chapter 25, Isaiah praises God for fulfilling a long-ago promise of destroying the city of an unnamed enemy. On the holy mountain of Sinai, the Lord will provide a banquet for the people. This is a reference to the messianic banquet, an image often used in Old Testament literature. On this mountain, the Lord will swallow up death, reversing the idea that death has swallowed up all the things of the earth. It is a time for rejoicing in the Lord, who saved the people.

In chapter 26, Isaiah sings a psalm about the "strong city," Jerusalem, which the Lord protects with walls and ramparts. The gates are opened to let in those who will eventually return. The Lord is an eternal rock for the people, who brings down the mighty under the feet of the poor. The people will wait for the dawn of a new day when the Lord's judgment will teach justice to all nations, but the wicked will refuse to learn this justice.

The people of Israel suffered like a woman in labor, but they gave birth to the wind, meaning they gave birth to nothing. The Lord, however, will raise the people from their death and give birth to a new beginning for the people.

In chapter 27, Isaiah speaks of the Lord punishing the powerful wicked forces and Leviathan, a mythical dragon of the sea, a symbol of the power of evil. The Lord protects and nurtures the vineyard of Israel, but the Lord will march against Israel if the people bring forth briars and thorns, that is, if they abandon the Lord. Israel will expiate its guilt by destroying the altars and idols, leaving the fortified cities of the wicked a barren pasture. The Lord will destroy the wicked nations from the Euphrates River to Egypt and gather the children of Israel from Assyria to Egypt like a farmer who harvests grain. The Israelites will again worship the Lord on the holy mountain in Jerusalem.

### *Lectio Divina*

Spent 8 to 10 minutes in silent contemplation of the following passage:

When Jesus speaks of the disasters coming upon the earth at the end of time, he has the good news about sending out angels to gather the elect from the ends of the earth. When he speaks of his passion and death, he always adds the good news of his resurrection. Just as the Lord offers hope to the people of Israel after calamities strike the nation, Jesus offers us hope in the midst of the greatest tragedies of our life. The message of God always ends with a message of hope.

✠ *What can I learn from this passage?*

## Day 4: Salvation for Israel and Judah (28—32)

In chapter 28, Isaiah speaks poetically in an oracle against the northern kingdom of Israel. Samaria, the capital of Ephraim, stood on a hill like a garland on a person's head. Isaiah speaks of a majestic garland in the northern kingdom of Israel and the drunkards of Ephraim, a reference to the people of Samaria and Israel who abandoned the Lord of Israel. The Lord sends one who is powerful (the Assyrians) sweeping over the land like a destructive storm that will inundate Samaria like a flood. The Lord will protect a remnant of the people during this invasion.

Isaiah turns his attention to the southern kingdom of Judah and the priests and prophets who are like drunkards, staggering from strong wine, confused and incapable of judging. They live in degradation, in vomit and filth. They ridicule Isaiah, portraying him as a babbling and unintelligible fool. The Lord will reply by speaking to them in a language they do not understand, the language of their captives, the Assyrians. Isaiah warns them that in making an alliance with Egypt against the Assyrians, the leaders of Judah made a covenant with death. The Lord is laying a stone in Zion as a firm foundation for salvation for those who believe, but many reject it. Their alliance with Egypt will not help them. The onslaught of the Assyrians shall continue to bring terror, but the Lord will help them as the Lord helped David defeat the Philistines.

Isaiah compares the Lord's dealing with people to that of a farmer. The plowman plants after he tills and levels the land. The crushing of the seed and grain is necessary, not to pulverize them but to prepare them. The Lord knows how to balance punishment and favor.

In chapter 29, the Lord declares that Ariel, a name for Jerusalem, will be captured as David captured the city much earlier (see 2 Samuel 5:6–9). The people will be so overwrought they will be like dead people speaking from their graves. All of a sudden, the Lord will defend the city, a defense that takes the form of a cosmic event, with thunder, earthquakes, storms, and fire.

Unfortunately, the people will be unable to understand the Lord's message because it is sealed against some and given to others who are unable to read it. Because the people honor the Lord only with their lips, the Lord will take away all wisdom and guidance. When people attempt to hide their plans from the Lord, they are like vessels saying the potter did not make them and does not understand them.

The day of redemption is coming when life will be restored to Israel. The deaf will hear the words of the sealed scroll, the eyes of the blind will see, the lowly will find joy, and the poor will rejoice in the Holy One of Israel. The tyrant, the scoffer, and the wicked shall cease, and the children of Jacob will be able to understand the Lord as their maker. They shall praise the Lord of Israel. The erring shall find understanding, and those who find fault will receive instruction.

In chapter 30, a later editor lists a number of oracles against the nations. In the first oracle, Isaiah addresses the rebellious people who seek to make an alliance with Egypt to rebel against the Assyrians. Instead of victory, they will experience shame.

A second oracle is against the Beasts of Negeb. Isaiah refers to Egypt by the name Rahab Sit-still. Rahab is a furious sea monster. Egypt sits still, unresponsive to Judah's request for help. Because the people refused to listen to Isaiah, they will be like a high wall that will crash to the ground like a potter's jar. The Lord tells them that by waiting calmly with trust, they would have been saved. Instead, they chose to put their trust in horses. The Lord predicts they will become so panicky a thousand will flee with the appearance of one warrior.

The Lord wishes to show mercy, bringing them the security of food and drink, teaching and guiding them when they ask for it, but they must destroy their idols. If they follow the Lord, they will prosper as the Lord rewards them with rain for the seed and broad acreage for their animals. The moon and sun will become brighter, and the Lord will heal their wounds.

For the Israelites, there will be singing as at a banquet, when all return to the mountain of the Lord (Zion). The Lord will shatter Assyria, and the trophet (a place of sacrifice to idols) is ready for the sacrificing of the king of Assyria. The Lord will set the fire.

In chapter 31, Isaiah warns against those who seek an alliance with Egypt, putting their trust in horses and chariots instead of the Lord. Just as the lion growling over its prey has no fear of the shepherds challenging it, so shall the Lord of hosts protect Mount Zion against the enemy. As a shield, the Lord will hover over Jerusalem like birds. Assyria will fall by the sword wielded by the Lord, and the leaders who are aligned with the king of Assyria will abandon him.

In chapter 32, Isaiah speaks of a Davidic king and princes who will rule with justice, shielding the people. All the wickedness of the past will be reversed. Those who deceived others will no longer be honored. The wicked are those who spoke against the Lord and did not provide for the hungry and thirsty. Those who are noble plan noble deeds.

Isaiah addresses the complacent women, warning them that in a little more than a year they will lose their sense of complacency when the harvest fails. They will strip themselves with only a loincloth to cover them. The land will be covered with thorns and briars.

A reversal will take place when the spirit from on high comes upon them, and the wilderness will become a garden as vast as a forest. Justice will bring peace, calm, and security forever. People will live in peace, security, and rest. Those who plant beside streams and let the ox and donkey roam freely are blessed.

### Lectio Divina

Spend 8 to 10 minutes in silent contemplation of the following passage:

At times, Jesus tells his disciples they receive the privilege of understanding his message, but those who do not accept him "may look and see but not perceive, and hear and listen but not understand" (Mark 4:12). When the Lord spoke through Isaiah the prophet, some of the leaders of the people listened, but they rejected Isaiah's message of doom. They refused to listen with faith, which led to their destruction.

✠ *What can I learn from this passage?*

## Day 5: Judgment and Deliverance (33—35)

Chapters 33 through 35 appear to come from an author later than First Isaiah. In chapter 33, Isaiah speaks of the destruction of the enemy and God's blessings on Israel. All will receive punishment equal to the destruction they caused others. The Lord promised help to those who wait for the dawn. The Israelite writers sometimes used the image of night as representing a time of darkness when the Israelites suffered, and the image of morning as a time of salvation, a new beginning. The Lord's voice scatters the nations, who flee in fear, leaving their belongings behind for the Israelites to plunder. The Israelites will then praise the Lord for blessing Zion with wealth, salvation, wisdom, knowledge, and fear of the Lord.

Isaiah prophesies about a future that promises to be a time of devastation for Assyria and a time of strength for Zion. A majestic king will appear, a reference to the future messianic king. Zion shall become a city of festivals and securely established like a tent with sturdy pegs. The Lord will be with them, surrounding them with rivers and wide streams that no enemy can navigate. The Lord who saves them is judge, lawgiver, and king. Those who are as weak as the blind and lame will claim the spoils.

An oracle against the warriors of Edom in chapter 34 describes the Lord's destruction on the people of Edom whose corpses will be so many they will send up a stench. Like the sword of the priests offering sacrifice, the sword of the Lord will be covered with blood, and the people and the animals shall soak the land with their blood. The land shall become like burning pitch, a smoking waste.

Chapter 35 paints an idealistic picture of hope and joy for the people of Judah. Where the Lord brought devastation to Edom in the previous chapter, the Lord now brings rejoicing to the people and blossoming to the land of Judah. The glory of the Lord will appear as the Lord gives strength to the weakened people of the exile who will return home. As a symbol of renewed life, the eyes of the blind shall see, the ears of the deaf shall hear, the lame shall walk, and the mute shall speak. In place of the wasted land described in the previous chapter, the deserts sands will become a pool, and a holy way leading to Jerusalem will be opened for the Israelites. Those ransomed from slavery will enter Zion singing for joy.

## *Lectio Divina*

Spend 8 to 10 minutes in silent contemplation of the following passage:

When Benedict XVI resigned as pope, the cardinals elected a Jesuit cardinal who took the name Francis in honor of St. Francis of Assisi. As St. Francis had done, Pope Francis stressed the need to care for the poor and promised that caring for the poor would be a hallmark of his papacy. Since the election of Pope Francis, the concern and care for the poor reached the farthest ends of the world. Just as the words of Francis brought hope to the poor, so the Words of the Lord concerning the eventual renewal of the land bring hope to the Israelites.

✠ *What can I learn from this passage?*

---

### Day 6: Historical Appendix (36—39)

With the exception of chapter 38:9–20 and some other additions and omissions, the text follows closely the same situation found in 2 Kings 18:13—20:19. In the fourteenth year of King Hezekiah, Sennacherib, the king of Assyria, captured many of the fortified cities of Judah. He sent his commander and two companions to speak with Hezekiah in the city of Jerusalem, which the Assyrians had not yet captured.

Knowing that Egypt was too weak to offer support, the commander of the Assyrians sarcastically asks Hezekiah if he really believes Egypt will help him. He declares that Hezekiah lost the support of the gods when he destroyed the unsanctioned places where the Lord of Israel was worshiped by people of Judah. The king wanted Jerusalem to be the only sanctuary of the Lord in the land of Judah. The Assyrian king claims to have the support of the Lord. For the Assyrians, worshiping the God of Israel along with other gods was acceptable. They rejected the idea that the God of Israel was the only God.

The commander speaks to the people, telling them not to listen to Hezekiah, who was deceiving them, and not to trust in the Lord for victory as Hezekiah requested. He urges the Israelites to surrender to the Assyrians, promising to give them food and drink. He tells them the king of Assyria would lead them to a land similar to the land in which they were living. The people remain silent, as Hezekiah ordered them to do.

After the deputies of the king of Assyria left, Hezekiah sends word to Isaiah about the disgrace that Jerusalem is about to endure at the hands of the Assyrians. Isaiah tells Hezekiah's servants not to fear. Hezekiah then begs the Lord, the Creator and King of all the nations, to save him from the Assyrians who had destroyed the gods and idols of other nations.

Isaiah brings the Lord's response to Hezekiah's prayer. Because the Assyrians brag about their conquests, unaware of the help given them by the Lord of the Israelites, the Lord will force them to leave without conquering Jerusalem. The Lord promises that in two years the survivors of the house of Judah will again bear fruit. For the sake of the Lord's name and for the sake of David, the Lord's servant, the Lord will shield and protect the city.

That night, an angel of the Lord kills 185,000 men of the Assyrian army. Some commentators believe the Assyrian army was decimated by a plague. Sennacherib, the king of Assyria, returns home and, as he worships in the temple of his god, is killed by his sons.

In chapter 38, as Hezekiah is near death, he weeps and prays to the Lord. Isaiah later tells him that the Lord witnessed his tears and heard his prayer and that he would live fifteen more years. The Lord also promises to rescue him and the city from the hands of the king of Assyria and to protect the city like a shield for the sake of David and for the Lord's own sake.

At the news of Hezekiah's recovery, an envoy from Babylon comes to Jerusalem. Hezekiah, pleased with their arrival, shows them all the treasures of the city. Isaiah later asks what he showed them, and Hezekiah admits that he showed them everything. Isaiah predicted that the day is coming when everything will be carried off to Babylon, including Hezekiah's descendants who will be made attendants to the king of Babylon.

## *Lectio Divina*

Spend 8 to 10 minutes in silent contemplation of the following passage:

The Lord punished the Assyrians and Hezekiah for bragging about their successes, as though they succeeded without any help from the Lord. Paul the Apostle speaks about true boasting when he writes, "Whoever boasts, should boast in the Lord" (2 Corinthians 10:18). All the good we do in the world does not come from our own powers but from the power of the Lord working through us.

✠ *What can I learn from this passage?*

## *Review Questions*

1. Why does the Lord become angry with Assyria after the Lord made them a rod to punish the people of Israel?
2. Why does the Lord allow Israel and Judah to be ravaged?
3. Why did Judah seek an alliance with Egypt?
4. Who is the servant spoken about in the Book of Isaiah?

# The Book of Isaiah (III)

## ISAIAH 40—55

*Here is my servant whom I uphold, my chosen one with whom I am pleased. Upon him I have put my spirit; he shall bring forth justice to the nations (42:1).*

**Opening Prayer** (SEE PAGE 16)

## Context

**Part 1: Isaiah 40—42** Commentators refer to chapters 40 through 55 of Isaiah as written by Second Isaiah, not the same Isaiah who prophesied throughout chapters 1 through 39. The author of First Isaiah prophesied during the eighth century before Christ, while Second Isaiah prophesied during the sixth century before Christ. The book appears to have been written toward the end of the Babylonian exile. The author predicts the triumph of Cyrus of Persia over Babylon, under whom the Judeans will be permitted to return home.

**Part 2: Isaiah 43—55** The chapters speak prophetically of the future redemption and restoration of the people and land of Judah. The author pictures Cyrus of Persia as an instrument of the Lord, who will bring freedom to the Israelites by destroying Babylon. The Lord calls to Jerusalem to rejoice on the day the people return home and prosper.

Read aloud Isaiah 40—42.

### 40:1–31 Comfort and Deliverance

A sudden change of style and content take place as the author of Second Isaiah writes while in exile, with his focus on the future. The opening scene takes place in a heavenly council being held by the Lord. The Lord speaks of comfort for the people of Israel, whose guilt is expiated and who will now receive comfort and deliverance from exile. In the heavenly council, a voice proclaims that a straight path shall be made through the wilderness, indicating the return of the Israelites will not follow the path the traders take to Jerusalem but will find a more direct route as the Lord fills in the valleys, lowers the hills and mountains, and makes the rugged path smooth.

A voice directs the prophet to proclaim symbolically that Babylon is like grass and flowers that wither. The prophet is to shout out the good news of deliverance to the people, proclaiming the power of the Lord, who comes like a shepherd to the flock of the Israelites in exile. He asks who has measured the waters, the heavens, brought dust to the earth, or weighed the mountains and the hills. Who instructed or counseled the Lord? The obvious answer is that no one on earth has done this.

Compared to the Lord, all the nations are like a wisp or a cloud on a scale, like a drop in the bucket. There is no one to compare with the Lord, not even an empty idol that depends on a human being to carve or cast it. From the beginning of God's revelation to the Israelites, the people learned about the Lord, who is above the heavens and has power over princes and rulers.

### 41:1–29 The Liberation of Israel

From the east will come a champion of justice, a reference to Cyrus, the Persian leader, who is not named here. He battles with no casualties and moves swiftly. Although people of the coastlands fear the advance of this new, powerful army, the Israelites have no need to fear, for the Lord is with them. Those who oppress the Israelites will perish in shame. The Lord will grasp the hand of the Israelites, leading them with a promise of help. The Holy One of Israel will redeem the offspring of Jacob. The afflicted Israelites will find an abundance of water and a new life in their land.

The Lord addresses the false gods, telling them to present their case as though they were on trial. The Lord challenges them to predict the future to prove they are truly gods or to do something that will lead the people to reverence them with awe or fear. Since the gods are nothing, choosing to worship them would be considered an abomination before the Lord. The false gods are as empty as the wind.

### 42:1–25 The Servant of the Lord

The Lord speaks of an unnamed servant. Although it is not clear whether the reference is to a group or an individual, it may be a reference to Israel. This reading is one of a group of psalms known as the "servant of the Lord psalms" (see also 49:1–7, 50:4–11, 52:13—53:12). Unlike violent conquerors, the servant shall receive the spirit of the Lord. The Lord adds the servant will not break a bruised reed, a sign that the mission of the servant is to bring peace and gentleness. The Lord has chosen Israel to bring a new covenant of justice between all people and God. Israel shall be a light for the nations to bring salvation to the blind, the prisoners, and those who live in the darkness of sin and error.

The Lord, like a warrior who has kept silent, now cries out the battle cry, gasping and panting like a woman in labor, intent on protecting the people of God. The Lord will lead the Israelites back to their homeland, making their path straight by removing mountains and hills, changing rivers into marshes, leading the weak and blind, and making darkness light.

The Lord will destroy those who worship idols and will aid the Israelites, plundered by the enemy, trapped in holes, and imprisoned. In the past, the Lord abandoned the Israelites to the plunderers because of the sins they committed in refusing to follow the Lord's teachings. Even in their destruction they did not realize their devastation was a result of their sinfulness.

# Review Questions

1. What is important about the Lord's Words of salvation in chapter 40?
2. Who is the servant of the Lord in the era of Isaiah?
3. Why does the Lord tell the people to sing to the Lord a new song?

## Closing Prayer (SEE PAGE 16)

Pray the closing prayer now or after *lectio divina*.

## Lectio Divina (SEE PAGE 9)

Relax your body and maintain a posture of prayer (back straight, eyes shut, feet flat on the floor). This exercise can take as long as you want, but in the context of this Bible study, 10 to 20 minutes should be sufficient.

The meditations that follow are provided only to help group participants use this prayer form, but note that *lectio* is intended to bring one to a place of prayerful contemplation where the Word of God speaks to the hearer from his or her heart. (See page 9 for further instruction.)

### Comfort and Deliverance (40:1–31)

On the day Jesus ascended into heaven, he promised to be with people "until the end of the age" (Matthew 28:20). In Second Isaiah, we read that even though young men may grow weary, the Lord never does. As the source of all knowledge and goodness, the Lord is always protecting and guiding us until the end of time. Our duty is to trust the loving power and endurance of God in our life.

✠ *What can I learn from this passage?*

### The Liberation of Israel (41:1–29)

Many of the Israelites believed in the Lord of Israel, but in their ignorance, they also wanted to avoid upsetting another god who may really exist, so they added some false gods to their worship just in case. The Lord views this wavering between the gods as an abomination.

In our world today, we may not be as generous as we should be because we worry about securing our future. The desire for assurance can drive many people to worship false gods. Jesus says, "Do not worry about tomorrow;

tomorrow will take care of itself" (Matthew 6:34). Securing our future is not something bad, but we must not allow it to destroy our trust in the Lord or overshadow our need to generously share our goods with those in need.

✠ *What can I learn from this passage?*

### The Servant of the Lord (42:1–25)

Although Second Isaiah does not name the servant of the Lord, those who serve the Lord receive the call to follow the example of the servant. In the New Testament era, many early Church writers viewed Jesus as the Suffering Servant who declared he was bringing peace into the world, even at the cost of his life. The image of the servant of the Lord could apply to each one of us who also receive the call to bring peace and justice in the world, whatever the cost.

✠ *What can I learn from this passage?*

## PART 2: INDIVIDUAL STUDY (ISAIAH 43—55 )

### Day 1: Redemption and Restoration (43—44:23)

The Lord tells those who are chosen not to fear, promising to be with them as they pass through rivers without being swept away and through fire without being burned. Because the Lord loves the Israelites, the Lord gives nations such as Egypt and Seba (Arabia) to the plunderers in place of Israel. The Lord will bring back to Judah all the Israelites from the north, the south, and all ends of the earth. All nations will witness the salvation brought to Israel through the power of the God of Israel. No god existed before or after the Lord, who is the one true Savior. When the Lord acts, no one can act against the Lord.

For the sake of the Israelites, the Lord will destroy the defenses of Babylon. The Lord is the one true God, the Redeemer and Creator. The destruction of the Babylonians recalls the destruction of the Egyptians in the Book of Exodus as they attempted to pass through the Red Sea in pursuit of Moses and the Israelites (see Exodus 14—15). The Lord opened a path through the sea for the Israelites and destroyed the Egyptian army, so the Lord will protect the Israelites while chariots and horsemen of the Babylonian army will be overwhelmed by the waters of the Lord's wrath.

The Lord instructs the Israelites not to remember the events of the past but to recognize the Lord is bringing about something new. The Lord blessed the Israelites in the past to encourage them in their worship of the Lord, but they grew weary of worshiping and offering sacrifices. They were a sinful people from the beginning, and the Lord, in retaliation, exposed Israel to destruction and the scorn of the nations.

In chapter 44, the Lord continues to repeat that Jacob should not fear, and the Lord will provide water for his people, filling them and their descendants with the spirit of the Lord. The promise of the Lord toward the descendants of Abraham recalls the Words of the Lord to Abraham, promising a blessing on his descendants (see Genesis 12:1–3). The Israelites shall prosper like poplar trees alongside flowing waters. The Lord is the first and the last, beside whom there is no other. The Lord challenges those who would dare to say that their gods are like the Lord of the Israelites. The Lord is the only one who can claim to be a rock to the people.

The Lord points out the foolishness of worshiping gods made by human beings. Artisans, who fashion iron images of the gods, make a form from the coals, shaping it with a hammer and a strong arm. The creator is a mere human being who grows hungry when his strength declines and grows thirsty and faint. The woodworker uses the same wood in carving a god that he uses to keep himself warm and to bake bread and to roast meat. In contrast, the Lord calls on the people of Israel to recognize the Creator who shaped them as the one true God of Israel, who will never forget them. All the earth will proclaim the Lord has redeemed Israel. The one Lord and God of Israel is not one god among many, but the one and only God.

### Lectio Divina

Spend 8 to 10 minutes in silent contemplation of the following passage:

In the Book of Exodus, the Lord gives Moses the first commandment, "You shall not have other gods beside me. You shall not make for yourself an idol or likeness of anything in the heavens above or on the earth below or in the waters beneath the earth" (Exodus 20:3–4).

In Isaiah, the Lord points out the foolishness of worshiping idols that are the work of human hands and will later wear out and corrode. The Lord realized people would have difficulty choosing the one true God over the false gods of pride, greed, pleasure, and other earthly allurements that will not endure. The struggle continues today, in our own lives.

✠ *What can I learn from this passage?*

## Day 2: The Agent of Israel's Deliverance (44:24—45:25)

In the following passages, Lord predicts Jerusalem will again be inhabited and the cities of Judah will be rebuilt, and the one to fulfill the Lord's wishes will be none other than Cyrus, whom the Lord speaks of as "my shepherd" (44:28).

In chapter 45, Cyrus receives the title of the Lord's anointed, which is used to identify a person specially chosen to act for the Lord. The Lord leads Cyrus to victory after victory, like a parent who grasps the hand of a child. Cyrus will shatter bronze doors and snap iron bars, an image that points to the gates of the fortifications of Babylon that were protected by bronze doors, and he will capture the treasures of Babylon. Although Cyrus does not know the God of the Israelites, it is the Lord of the Israelites who will guide him, the Lord who is the Creator of all that exists in the heavens and on earth.

After speaking of the salvation and justice for the Israelites, the Lord predicts misery for those who dare to contend with the Maker of creation. Just as clay should not complain to the potter that his work is incomplete, so no one should complain to the Lord about the Lord's children. The Lord chooses Cyrus to rebuild the city of Jerusalem and bring freedom to the exiles, while receiving no payment in return. No one should complain to the Lord.

All those who carve false images are disgraced as nations recognize the Lord has saved Israel. The Lord, the Creator, created the world out of chaos, out of an empty waste. When the people see the salvation brought by God, they must proclaim the Lord, who was with them from the beginning, is the one just and saving God.

The Lord calls upon all people to turn and worship the one and only true God. All shall recognize the greatness of the Lord, and those who once rejected the Lord will come and worship the God of the Israelites. The descendants of Israel shall receive vindication and will glory in the triumph of the Lord.

### *Lectio Divina*

Spend 8 to 10 minutes in silent contemplation of the following passage:

Centuries ago, the Lord chose the family of Abraham. Since that time, some of the Israelites became indifferent and encountered many afflictions throughout the centuries, but somehow the nation survives to this day. People may abandon the covenant made with the Lord, but the Lord will never break the covenant made with the people.

The Lord made a covenant with the Church in the person of Jesus Christ. Amazingly, the Church, like the Israelites, survived periods in history when it should have collapsed, but it did not. Throughout history, the Lord remains faithful to the covenant, even when those under the covenant do not live as they should. The Lord keeps calling us back to living our part of the covenant faithfully, protecting and guiding us so those of us who offend the Lord can find our way back to holiness.

✠ *What can I learn from this passage?*

---

## Day 3: The Fall of Babylon (46—48)

The ancients often saw battles between nations as a battle between the gods. The gods of Babylon, Bel, and Nebo will go into captivity, a sign they are less powerful and false gods. The Lord of Israel would eventually prove to be the one true and powerful God. There are gods made of gold and silver who are carried and set in a place but who do not answer or save the nations from distress. The Lord of Israel summons from the east a bird of prey, a reference to Cyrus who comes from Persia. Those who are fainthearted, who doubted, will recognize the power of the Lord when the Lord brings salvation to Israel.

In chapter 47, the Lord speaks of the fall of the once mighty Babylon, which will sit in the dust, stripped naked (as conquerors did to prisoners), with no relief from the fate of the captured, no possibility of entering a treaty with their conquerors. The nation will go into darkness, sit meekly in silence, and suffer the humiliation of falling from grandeur.

The Lord became angry with Babylon because the Babylonians showed no mercy to the people they conquered. They believed they were invincible and boasted they would never be like a widow without children. In a single day, when they are conquered, they will grieve like childless widows, and they will find no help in their gods and their spells. They said with pride, "I, and no one else" (47:10), and in saying this, they were opposing the God of the Israelites, who is the one true God. The Lord derides their belief in the false gods, noting all their sorcerers, astrologers, and stargazers are like useless stubble consumed by fire.

In chapter 48, the Lord exhorts the Israelite exiles to recognize their past sins. They swear by the name of the Lord and call upon the God of Israel, but they are insincere and unjust. The Lord warned them long ago, and suddenly he put the warnings into action, knowing the Israelites were a stubborn people. The Lord spoke to them in the past to keep them from viewing idols, statues, or molten images as their protectors and helpers. Now, as they see what is happening in bringing them to freedom, they must admit the guidance of the one true God.

The Lord knows the Israelites were rebels who refused to listen, but despite the Lord's anger the Lord did not destroy them for the sake of the name of the Lord. The Lord refined them and tested them in a furnace of suffering so all nations would glorify the name of the Lord. The Lord called Cyrus and made him successful.

The Lord speaks to the Israelites, proclaiming again the Lord is the Holy One of Israel who teaches and leads them. The Lord repeats the promise made to Abraham that the offspring of the Israelites will be as numerous as the sands and their names shall never be blotted out from the presence of the Lord (see Genesis 22:17). Just as the people of Israel escaped from Egypt and journeyed through the wilderness under the leadership of Moses, so the people of Israel shall experience God's blessings in their flight from Babylon, receiving water in the wilderness on their journey (see Exodus 17:1–7).

### *Lectio Divina*

Spend 8 to 10 minutes in silent contemplation of the following passage:

Trusting in God is difficult for people who are surrounded by the enemy or who are living in slavery, yet the Book of Isaiah keeps reminding us the Lord may allow suffering, not because the Lord loves to see us suffer but to cleanse our hearts. No matter how difficult life becomes, the Lord offers us strength to endure. Jesus called us to this trust when he said, "Do not let your hearts be troubled. You have faith in God; have faith also in me" (John 14:1). In writing about salvation coming to the Israelites, Isaiah offers the nation hope, and the foundation of hope is faith in God. With trust in God, we can learn to keep our hearts from being troubled.

✠ *What can I learn from this passage?*

---

## Day 4: Salvation Through the Lord's Servant (49—50)

The following passage is the second of the servant songs found in the Book of Isaiah. The message of the Lord reaches out as far as the coastlands, implying it is a message for the whole world. Although the passage names Israel as the Lord's servant, the broader text seems to point to an individual or a group within Israel called to share the glory of Israel and to serve Israel.

The Lord chose the servant from the time the servant was in his mother's womb. The tongue of the servant was like a sharp-edged sword with the mission of proclaiming the Lord's message to all nations. In his efforts to proclaim faithfulness to the Lord, the servant may have felt his efforts amounted to nothing. Because the Lord is with him, he believes the Lord will bring Israel back to faith in their Redeemer. The servant receives a call to reach out beyond Israel, to bring the Lord's message of salvation to the entire world, to act as a light to the nations. Israel was a nation despised and enslaved by foreign rulers, but now kings and princes shall treat Israel with respect, because they will recognize Israel has been chosen by the Holy One of Israel.

The Lord set Cyrus as a covenant of freedom for the people of Israel. He will restore the land of Israel and release prisoners from exile. Their journey to the homeland shall be filled with pastures, even where the heights were once barren. The Lord, who has compassion on them, will provide food and water, protect them from the scorching wind and sun, lower the mountains, and make the highways level. Israelites from all ends of the earth will return home. The heavens and mountains sing and the earth rejoices when they encounter the comfort and mercy the Lord shows to the people of Israel.

When the people of Israel recall their discouragement in exile, believing the Lord had forgotten about them, the Lord responds, asking if a mother could forget her child. Even if she could, the Lord can never abandon Israel. When the day of freedom comes, all Israelites will come to Israel in haste. The large number of those returning will show the nation has not died in exile but has increased wherever the Israelites settle among the nations. The Lord declares kings shall be the guardians of those returning, and princesses shall be their nursemaids. Other nations shall pay homage to Israel. Captives and plunder will be returned. The Lord will oppose those who oppose the Israelites, forcing them to eat the flesh of their own army and drink their blood. All nations will recognize the Lord of Israel as the savior and redeemer of the people of Israel.

In chapter 50, the Lord, reminding the complaining Israelites the covenant was still in existence, asks where the bill of divorce was that separated the people from the Lord, or the creditors receipt declaring the Lord has sold the people. When the Lord called upon the people to remain faithful, no one answered the call. The hand of the Lord is not too short to deliver judgment. The Lord can still dry up the sea, turn rivers into wilderness, and clothe the heavens in black. The last image recalls the darkness that covered the land during the plagues in Egypt when the Pharaoh of Egypt refused to allow Moses and the Israelites to leave his country (see Exodus 10:21–29).

The servant of the Lord will declare the Lord has given him a well-informed tongue to speak to the weary Israelites and to inspire them to action. The Lord God spoke to the servant who willingly received the call and all it entailed. He accepted being whipped, having his beard torn out, and other punishments. The servant trusts in the help of the Lord, ashamed of nothing, firm in following the Lord. Since the Lord is his help, who would dare declare him guilty? Those who walk in darkness and trust the Lord are the ones who show a reverential fear of the Lord. Those who believe they walk by their own enlightenment, walking by the light of their own fire, shall lie down in a place of torment.

### Lectio Divina

Spend 8 to 10 minutes in silent contemplation of the following passage:

The servant of the Lord accepts every form of humiliation and suffering, as Jesus did. Jesus calls his followers to be willing to suffer for his sake. Isaiah proclaims those who walk in darkness without any light, yet who trust in the Lord, are the ones who have a reverential fear and love of the Lord.

✠ *What can I learn from this passage?*

## Day 5: Trust in the Lord (51—53)

The Lord calls upon Israel to look to the rock from which they were hewn. The rock is the ancestry of the Israelites such as Abraham and Sarah. The Lord blessed them with a large number of offspring. The Lord will comfort the people of Israel, making her wilderness as lush as Eden, a garden of the Lord. A spirit of joy, thanksgiving, and song shall be found among them.

The Lord declares victory against Babylon will come quickly, bringing salvation to Israel and judgment to the nations. Although the heavens, earth, and many of the earth's inhabitants will pass away, the Lord's salvation will last forever. Those who know true justice and accept the teachings of the Lord with their whole heart have no need to fear the reproaches of others who are like garments consumed by moths and worms. The Lord urges the Israelites to wake up, reminding them they once conquered the power of Egypt, represented in Isaiah as Rahab, a dragon sea monster. Those ransomed by the Lord will joyfully return to Zion, where all sadness and mourning will end. The Israelites feared the oppressive Babylonian army, but the Lord asks where the oppressor's fury is now. The Lord declares that the captives will soon be freed and well fed.

The Lord urges on Jerusalem, who drank the cup of the Lord's wrath down to the dregs and who once had many children but now has none.

Without anyone left to grieve over Jerusalem, the suffering is even greater. Desolation, famine, and the sword left no one to give comfort to Jerusalem. Her children are as helpless as an antelope caught in a net. The Lord speaks to a people who are drunk with suffering, not wine. Jerusalem shall no longer drink of the wrath of God. Instead, those who tormented the Israelites and forced them to grovel so the tormentors could walk over them will now experience the Lord's wrath.

The Lord again calls the people of Zion to wake up, become strong again, and attire themselves in the splendid garments of power and peace. No longer shall the uncircumcised (Gentile enemies) or unclean enter the city of Jerusalem. Jerusalem is to move from a nation groveling in the dust to one enthroned above other nations. The Lord sold the nation into slavery in exile, and the Lord redeems it without cost.

The prophet portrays the joy of the one who brings the good news of salvation to the people as proof that the Lord of Israel is truly king. The sentinels (prophets) raise a joyful shout when they see the Lord has returned to protect Zion. All nations and all ends of the earth see the salvation brought by the mighty arm of the Lord. The Lord directs the people to depart from their exile, not touching anything unclean. Those who carry the vessels of the Lord are to purify themselves. Since the Lord goes before and after them, there is no need to leave in haste.

In the last oracles of the servant of the Lord, the Lord declares God's servant shall prosper and be greatly exalted, as many people and kings marvel at the change of the servant from his horrible state of oppression to his exaltation.

Chapter 53 continues the suffering servant oracle. The servant, who grew up in a normal manner with no majestic bearing or beauty making him stand out, experienced rejection and knew pain through his own suffering. He bore the suffering of the people, stricken down by the Lord, pierced, and crushed for the guilt of the people. In receiving a punishment for the sake of the people, he brought them healing. Like straying sheep, the people abandoned the Lord, and the servant bore their sins. In silence, he accepted his punishment on their behalf like a sheep led to slaughter or a sheep being sheared.

The servant received condemnation from his accusers, and they buried him with the wicked, although he had done nothing wrong. It was the Lord's will, however, that he should be crushed with pain to make reparation for the people. Many others will follow his example, even after his death. Despite his suffering and pain, he will conquer for the sake of the people. The author pictures the servant as a conqueror who divides the spoils with those who are strong.

### Lectio Divina

Spend 8 to 10 minutes in silent contemplation of the following passage:

Many commentators view the afflictions endured by the suffering servant and the meekness of the servant before his accusers as a foreshadowing of Jesus, the suffering servant of the Lord who brought salvation to the world. He silently endured suffering for our sake to the point of dying for us, but he was raised, and with him we were raised to a new life in Christ. For Christians, Jesus is the suffering servant foreshadowed in the Book of Isaiah.

✠ *What can I learn from this passage?*

---

## Day 6: The New Zion (54—55)

Isaiah incites Jerusalem, who was like a barren wife, to rejoice and sing because now the city will see many children born anew in the holy city. Jerusalem shall expand her borders like one who would enlarge a tent for a larger family, possessing the land of the surrounding nations. The shame of Jerusalem shall cease, and people will forget the devastation of the city. The city's husband is the Maker of the city, the Lord of hosts, redeemer, the Holy One of Israel, and God of all the earth.

The Lord admits abandoning the people for a brief time, but now the Lord lovingly calls them back, recalling the days of Noah when the Lord swore never to flood the earth again. The Lord swears never to be angry with the people or rebuke them. Although the mountains and hills may disappear, the love of the Lord and the Lord's covenant of peace will never be shaken.

The nation will be just, with no fear of oppression or destruction. Those who attack will be defeated, since the attack does not come from the Lord.

All weapons fashioned against them shall fail, and their accusers shall be proven liars.

In chapter 55, the Lord invites the people to a banquet, providing drink for those who are thirsty and food for those who are without funds. The Lord calls for complete trust, urging the people to spend their money on food and the necessities of life. The Lord offers to make an eternal covenant with the people, extending the covenant made with David. For the deliverance of the Israelites, the Lord will summon a nation the people did not know, apparently Persia, and that nation shall offer speedy help to Jerusalem. This nation may also be a generic reference to many nations.

The Lord calls upon the wicked to abandon their evil ways and turn to the Lord, who is merciful and forgiving. Just as the rain and snow come from the heavens without returning there until they have watered the earth and made it fruitful, so the Word of the Lord will not return to the Lord empty but will achieve the good for which it was sent.

The Lord directs the Israelites to go forth in peace. Second Isaiah pictures the journey home to Judah as a joyful and triumphant journey. All nature will rejoice, including mountains, hills, and trees, with cypress trees replacing thornbushes and myrtle growing instead of nettles. This return to Jerusalem shall redound to the glory of the Lord, an eternal sign that will never fail.

### Lectio Divina

Spend 8 to 10 minutes in silent contemplation of the following passage:

When the Israelites lived in exile, wondering why the Lord appeared to be sleeping and unresponsive to their needs, they suddenly receive word the Lord will bring them to freedom. In our life, the Lord may appear to be asleep, but Jesus promises to be with us in the midst of the storms in our life. The Lord is always awake, ready to help us in our needs.

✠ *What can I learn from this passage?*

## *Review Questions*

1. What comparison does the Lord make between the presence of the Lord God among the people of Judah and false gods?

2. How could Cyrus of Persia be an agent of the Lord when he worships other gods?

3. Why does the Lord call Zion to wake up?

## LESSON 4

# The Book of Isaiah (IV)

### ISAIAH 56—66

*Raise your eyes and look about; they all gather and come to you—Your sons from afar, your daughters in the arms of their nurses. Then you shall see and be radiant, your heart shall throb and overflow. For the riches of the sea shall be poured out before you, the wealth of nations shall come to you (60:4–5).*

**Opening Prayer** (SEE PAGE 16)

## Context

**Part 1: Isaiah 56—58** Commentators refer to chapters 56 through 66 of Isaiah as Third Isaiah or Trito-Isaiah, and it appears to have been written after the return of the Israelites from exile in Babylon. Despite the positive promises of a peaceful settlement in Israel as found in Second Isaiah and the promise that the Lord will never leave them, Third Isaiah deals with the hardships and hopes of those who returned, and God's expectations for the people of Israel.

**Part 2: Isaiah 59—66** These chapters speak of the final salvation of the Israelites, which brings joy and thanksgiving to the lips of the people. The Lord has come to rescue those who are faithful and reject those who are not. The Lord will bring about a renewed world, a new heaven and a new earth, bringing prosperity to Judah and bringing all nations to honor her.

## PART 1: GROUP STUDY (ISAIAH 56—58)

Read aloud Isaiah 56—58.

### 56:1–12 The Demands of the Covenant

The Lord stresses some commands of the covenant. The just person lives in the Lord's presence, not profaning the Sabbath and avoiding evil. Previously, certain tribes and those who were sexually mutilated were excluded; now foreigners and eunuchs should join the people of God (see Deuteronomy 23:2–9). The Lord will bring to the holy mountain and into the Lord's house those who keep the Sabbath and remain faithful to the covenant. The Lord's house is a house of prayer for all people. Many foreigners, referred to by the Israelites as beasts, will find salvation along with the people of Judah. The sentinels of Israel (the false prophets) are blind, lacking all knowledge.

### 57:1–21 An Idolatrous People

The Lord speaks of those who worship idols as children of a sorceress, offspring of an adulterer, and prostitutes. Prophets consider Israelites who worshiped false gods as prostituting themselves. The Lord addresses them as rebellious children, devious offspring who burn with lust and sacrifice children. They gather smooth stones from the wadi and use these stones as their idols, offering wine and grain to honor them. They sacrifice their firstborn male child to their king, Molech (a Canaanite deity), and offer oil and many perfumes to the deity. They send their ambassadors (the sacrificed children) down to death in Sheol.

The Lord asks if the people expect the Lord to remain silent when the people show no fear of the true God of Israel. When they are in danger and cry out, the Lord tells them to let their gods save them. Those who take refuge in the Lord shall inherit the land and possess the Lord's holy mountain, that is, they shall live in the peace of Jerusalem.

When the Lord, in anger, struck the Israelites and hid from them, they followed the yearning of their hearts and turned back to the Lord. When the Lord saw their change of heart, the Lord consoled them. The wicked, however, endure affliction that is like the churning of the sea, casting up mire and mud that leaves the wicked with no peace.

### 58:1–14 True Fasting

The people, believing they are following the law by fasting, ask why the Lord does not help them when they fast. The Lord berates the Israelites; while they fulfill the law of fasting, they do it with quarreling and fighting. The Lord declares the people make gestures of bowing low before the Lord and lying in sackcloth and ashes, but real fasting consists of releasing those unjustly bound and bringing freedom to those who are oppressed. Fasting is not a matter of external actions. Rather, it demands a spirit of fasting from oppressing others as well as fasting from food and drink.

True fasting, says the Lord, consists in sharing one's bread with the hungry, sheltering the oppressed and homeless, clothing the naked, and not turning one's back on a neighbor. If the Israelites fast in this manner, the nation will shine like the morning light, and the afflictions of their exile will be quickly healed. The Lord will answer their cry, removing oppression, false accusations, and wicked speech from their midst.

The Lord states that as long as the Israelites honor the Sabbath, avoiding their own evil pursuits, they will find delight in the Lord, and the Lord will raise them up, nourishing them with the legacy of Jacob, the father of the nation. As a binding seal on all that has been said, Isaiah ends this oracle by stating the Lord has spoken.

## Review Questions

1. Why is it important for the people of Judah to welcome the foreigners or eunuchs who profess faith in the Lord?
2. Who are the sinful shepherds?
3. What is the authentic fasting the Lord requires?

---

**Closing Prayer** (SEE PAGE 16)

Pray the closing prayer now or after *lectio divina*.

### Lectio Divina (SEE PAGE 9)

Relax your body and maintain a posture of prayer (back straight, eyes shut, feet flat on the floor). This exercise can take as long as you want, but in the context of this Bible study, 10 to 20 minutes should be sufficient.

The meditations that follow are provided only to help group participants use this prayer form, but note that *lectio* is intended to bring one to a place of prayerful contemplation where the Word of God speaks to the hearer from his or her heart. (See page 9 for further instruction.)

## The Demands of the Covenant (56:1–12)

The Israelites sinned grievously by worshiping foreign gods, but the Lord easily forgives them when they live a life faithful to the covenant. In loving and accepting the mutilated, the poor, and the hungry, the Israelites prove themselves worthy of forgiveness. "Merciful and gracious is the Lord, slow to anger, abounding in mercy" (Psalm 103:8).

✠ *What can I learn from this passage?*

## An Idolatrous People (57:1–21)

Many of the Israelites have apparently accepted the horrible practice of sacrificing children instead of animals to the false gods. Earlier in history, when the Lord asked Abraham to sacrifice his son Isaac, the Lord at the last minute kept Abraham from making this type of sacrifice (see Genesis 22:1–19). The event illustrates the Lord does not condone human sacrifice. Although Jesus knew there would be times when his disciples must sacrifice their life for love of God or others, Jesus condemned the killing of another person. Jesus said, "No one has greater love than this, to lay down one's life for one's friends" (John 15:13). When Jesus died on the cross, he offered himself as a sacrifice for all of us.

✠ *What can I learn from this passage?*

## True Fasting (58:1–14)

According to the Lord, true sacrifices consist in external actions and in a personal commitment to love the Lord and others. In many ways, the Lord is speaking to us today. We could pray for many hours, worship every

Sunday with the community, and fast at the appointed times, but if we ignore or hurt our neighbor, all our apparently good actions mean nothing to the Lord. Our external actions and interior spirit must all be directed toward the love of the Lord and our neighbor.

✠ *What can I learn from this passage?*

---

## PART 2: INDIVIDUAL STUDY (ISAIAH 59—66)

---

### Day 1: Punishment and Salvation (59—60)

Isaiah lists the sins of the people. They are liars, cause havoc, hatch deeds of wickedness, weave webs of deceit, perform evil and violent acts, shed innocent blood, entertain wicked thoughts, plan violence and destruction, and reject deeds of peace and justice. They growl like bears and moan like doves, crying for justice and salvation that eludes them.

To the people of Zion who turn from their sinfulness, the Lord shall come as their redeemer. Like a warrior preparing for battle, the Lord puts on justice as a breastplate, victory as a helmet, and vengeance as a weapon against the nations according to their deeds. All wicked people, west and east, shall fear the name and glory of the Lord. The Lord will make a covenant with the Israelites that is really a renewal of the covenant the Lord made with the ancestors of the Israelites. The Israelites shall receive the spirit of the Lord, and the Word of the Lord will dwell with the people from generation to generation.

In chapter 60, the Lord speaks of a new beginning for Israel. In the midst of darkness and gloom hovering over the earth, the Lord will dawn on the Israelites, and Israel will become a light to the nations. The exiles who fled from Judah will return from a great distance. As sign of new life, nurses will carry the daughters of the Israelites in their arms. The prophet pictures a procession of camels, dromedaries, and a host of nations from Arabia, bringing precious gifts such as gold and frankincense, all praising the Lord of Israel.

People from foreign nations shall rebuild the walls of Jerusalem, and kings shall minister to the Israelites. Kings who follow Cyrus will continue to aid in the rebuilding of Jerusalem. Just as the Lord's wrath in the past struck some of the people, so the Lord will show mercy and restore the nation. The gates of the city, ordinarily kept closed to protect the nation against aggressors, will remain open to receive the wealth of the nations. The precious wood from Lebanon will bring glory to the sanctuary where the Lord dwells. The nations that once oppressed them will now acclaim Jerusalem to be the "City of the Lord" and "Zion of the Holy One of Israel" (Isaiah 60:14).

Like an infant, Israel will suck the milk of nations and be nursed at the royal breasts, treated by nations with the gifts and concern a mother shows to her child. The people of Israel will recognize the Lord, the Mighty One of Jacob, as their redeemer. They will receive precious metals of gold and silver, instead of wood and bronze, and will be governed by peace and justice, free from violence, plunder, and destruction. The city will be protected with walls of salvation and gates of praise.

The prophet proclaims the people will no longer need the light of the sun or moon, since the Lord will be their light and glory. In this light, grieving will end and justice will prevail. The shoot the Lord planted, namely Israel, will flourish. The Lord promises to accomplish this with haste when the time comes.

### Lectio Divina

Spend 8 to 10 minutes in silent contemplation of the following passage:

Matthew's Gospel quotes from Isaiah the prophet when Jesus chooses Capernaum in the region of Zebulun and Naphtali as his home base during his public ministry. With Jesus in their midst, "the people who sit in darkness have seen a great light" (Matthew 4:16). The presence of the Lord in the midst of the people is viewed as light in the darkness. In the same way, the Lord promises to be with the Israelites as a light in the darkest moments of their existence.

✠ *What can I learn from this passage?*

## Day 2: The Lord's Continual Protection (61—62)

The prophet receives the call to act under the guidance of the spirit of the Lord God. The coming of the spirit of the Lord upon the prophet signifies an anointing for his mission. He will bring the Lord's good news of salvation to the afflicted, encouragement to the brokenhearted, and freedom to prisoners, such as slaves captured in battle. He will announce a year of favor from the Lord, which is a year of forgiveness, allowing people to reclaim the land taken from them, and a year to allow the land to rest from sowing (see Leviticus 25:10–11). The prophet receives the call to comfort those who are mourning or grieving by crowning them with a wreath of joy instead of ashes and anointing them with the oil of happiness in place of mourning.

The prophet declares the Israelites will rebuild the ruins of Judah and restore the cities decimated by the Babylonians. People from other nations will work with the Israelites, pasturing their flocks, tending the farms and vineyards while referring to the Israelites as "Priests of the LORD" (61:6). This title recalls the Words of the Lord to Moses on Sinai: "You will be to me a kingdom of priests, a holy nation" (Exodus 19:6). The prophet adds the Israelites will be called "Ministers of our God" (61:6). Because the Israelites received twofold punishment from the Lord, they will receive a twofold abundance of possessions.

The Lord will renew the covenant made with the ancestors of the Israelites. Their offspring will be legendary among the nations, leading those who witness their blessings to proclaim that they are truly the offspring of the Lord. Third Isaiah, speaking in the name of Israel, joyfully glorifies the Lord for clothing the nation in garments of salvation and justice, as though the Israelites were a couple elegantly adorned for their wedding. Just as the earth produces its plants, so the Lord will make justice spring up for the Israelites.

In chapter 62, the Lord speaks with affection concerning the Israelites. For the sake of the Israelites, the Lord will not remain silent, which means the Lord will continue to protect the nation. The vindication and salvation of Israel will be like a burning beacon for the nations and their kings. Israel will be a glorious crown, a royal diadem, in the hand of the Lord. In the past the nation was known as "Forsaken," and their land "Desolate," but the Lord bestows on Israel a new name, "My Delight is in her," and their land "Espoused" (62:4). As a young man married a virgin, so the Lord, their Builder, shall marry them.

Day and night, the Lord will place sentinels on the walls of Jerusalem, a reference to the prophets who will protect the people with warnings and directions from the Lord. The prophet declares that the grain and wine harvested by the Israelites will no longer become food and drink for enemies. When armies such as the Assyrians or Babylonians invaded the land, these armies would gather the harvest for themselves and leave nothing for the inhabitants.

With the destruction of the Babylonian army, the Israelites pass through the gates of Babylon to freedom. Nations will recognize the Lord has visited and rewarded the people of Israel. In the sight of all nations, the Israelites shall be named "The Holy People," "The Redeemed of the LORD," "Cared For," "A City Not Forsaken" (62:12).

### *Lectio Divina*

Spend 8 to 10 minutes in silent contemplation of the following passage:

Christians believe the Lord has chosen them to be a "holy nation," a people who were once "no people, but now you are God's people" (1 Peter 2:9–10). Like the Israelites who were once forsaken and became the delight of the Lord, so Christians receive the call to live as the Lord's holy people. Bearing the name Christian is not enough. Holiness is the true sign of being a Christian.

✠ *What can I learn from this passage?*

## Day 3: Pleading for the Lord's Help (63—64)

A sentinel (a prophet) asks who is coming from Borah, the capital of Edom, in crimson-stained garments, gloriously attired, endowed with strength. The Lord is the one who is coming. Edom took advantage of the weakened condition of Judah after the Babylonian invasion of Jerusalem and plundered the Israelite cities. The Lord now announces vindication and salvation for the Israelites.

The sentinel asks why the Lord's garments are red. Apocalyptic language refers to the image of the winepress when speaking of a bloody destruction of enemies. The Lord in anger trods the winepress alone, with no one to help and with blood spurting on the Lord's garments. The Lord made the people drunk with the Lord's wrath and poured out their blood like useless wine on the ground.

The prophet recalls the loving deeds and actions the Lord performed for Israel. The Lord raised them up and carried them as the Lord did with their ancestors, but the Israelites rebelled, grieving the Lord. In retaliation, the Lord battled against them as their enemy.

The prophet, referring to the time the Lord led Moses and the Israelites through the sea, searches for the Lord whose spirit performed these mighty deeds. Where is the Lord who guided the Israelites through the wilderness with their horses and cattle? Where is the Lord's care and compassion for the people? The prophet prays that the Lord, who is their Father, not withhold mercy from them. They ask why the Lord allows them to wander from the Lord's commands and harden their hearts against the Lord. Some Old Testament writers believed the Lord was the one who hardened the hearts of people so they would not listen.

The prophet prays to the Lord for help for the sake of the Lord's concern for the tribes of Israel. The Lord has rejected them for too long. It is time for the Lord to break open the heavens and come down.

In chapter 64, the prophet declares the fame of the Lord of Israel blazes across the nation like a fire igniting brushwood or a fire making water boil. The unimaginable deeds of the Lord cause nations to tremble in fear of the Lord. The prophet laments the sinfulness of the Israelites, wishing the Lord would find them doing right instead of sinning and causing the Lord to be angry with them. The Israelites have become unclean, like contaminated rags and withering dry leaves that the wind blows away.

Despite acknowledging the abandonment by the Lord, the prophet appeals to the Lord as the father of the nation, declaring the Israelites are like clay in the hands of the Lord, the potter. Pointing to the devastation of Jerusalem and the fiery destruction of the Temple where their ancestors praised the Lord, the prophet asks how the Lord can remain silent and not act.

## *Lectio Divina*

Spend 8 to 10 minutes in silent contemplation of the following passage:

In the Gospel of Luke, Jesus says, "I have come to set the earth on fire, and how I wish it were already blazing!" (Luke 12:49). When Jesus notes his message will divide believers from nonbelievers, he admits he did not come to bring peace on earth but division, even within families. In Isaiah, the Lord's fame and words blaze from nation to nation like a consuming fire, striking fear and oppression into the hearts of those who do not believe in the Lord of Israel. Unfortunately, the world will always remain in conflict, with the followers of the Lord in conflict with those who do not believe.

✠ *What can I learn from this passage?*

---

## Day 4: The Fate of the Just and the Unjust in Israel (65—66)

Although the Israelites did not seek the Lord, the Lord responded to their plight by declaring, "Here I am! Here I am!" (65:1) and stretching out a loving hand to the people who chose to follow their own objectives rather than the Lord's. The people provoked the Lord and offered sacrifices in garden shrines and burned incense on bricks, which were considered sacred stones of idols. Following the practice of seeking omens from the dead, the people sat in tombs and spent nights in caves, eating the unclean food of pigs offered to idols and drinking their broth.

The prophet ridicules the people, picturing them as telling the Lord not to come near them lest they become holy. The Lord, confronted with such rejection on the part of the people, predicts the people will receive full payment for their sins and the sins of their ancestors. Because the people insulted the Lord by burning incense to false idols, the Lord will pour out a full measure of recompense into their laps. In ancient times, when people bought grain, the seller would pour out the grain into the lap of the garment of the buyer.

The Lord then uses the image of juice being pressed from a cluster of fruit. At that point, someone would say the crushed fruit on the cluster should not be destroyed, since there is still some good in it. In the same way, the Lord will destroy the people of Israel but not all of them. The Lord promises to bring forth offspring from the tribe of Judah who will obtain the land from Sharon, a northern coastal plain near Judah, to the Valley of Achor, a bleak region west of the Dead Sea. Those who reject the Lord and Jerusalem and worship "Fortune" and "Destiny," gods of favorable outcomes, will be destined for slaughter.

The Lord promises to save a remnant of the people. The remnant shall eat, drink, and shout for joy. The remnant not saved, however, shall suffer hunger, thirst, disgrace, and grief.

The Lord speaks of creating a new heaven and a new earth. With the new heaven and new earth, former events will no longer be remembered. The sound of weeping will cease as infants and the people live a long life. The centenarian shall be considered a youth, and anyone who dies before a hundred will be considered accursed. The people will build houses and live in them without fear of being cast out, and those who plant vineyards shall eat their fruit. The people shall not toil in vain, as they did when the Babylonians invaded the land and feasted on the produce planted by the Israelites. The imagery used in this passage appears to be an apocalyptic and idealistic image of the new life in store for the Israelites.

The Lord will bless the people and their offspring. Before they call upon the Lord, the Lord will provide for their needs. The wolf and lamb shall pasture together and the lion shall eat hay like the ox. This passage reflects the creation story in which the Lord creates all the animals and gives them green plants, not meat, for food (see Genesis 1:30). Similar to the creation story concerning the punishment of the serpent who tempted Eve, the serpent's food shall be dust (see Genesis 3:14). On the Lord's holy mountain, no one will cause harm or destruction.

Chapter 66 uses apocalyptic imagery when speaking of the heavens as the Lord's throne and the earth as the Lord's footstool. Since the Lord created everything, it is foolish for human beings to believe they can build a house where the Lord can rest. Although the Temple is the Lord's house for the Israelites, they believe the Lord, who created the world, has dominion over all, making all the earth the house of the Lord.

The Lord praises those who show a reverential fear of the Lord and rejects those who abuse Temple worship. Although some fulfill lawful forms of sacrifice such as sacrificing an ox or a lamb, they also sacrifice a human being (apparently a reference to child sacrifice) and a dog or a pig to idols while burning incense in honor of an idol. They refuse to listen to the Lord and pursue what is evil in the Lord's sight. In the end, those who rebel shall be disgraced. The voice of the Lord, resounding from the holy city and the Temple, will bring retribution to the Lord's enemies.

The Lord pictures Zion as a woman about to give birth. Without the pains of labor, Zion gives birth to a land and a nation that is miraculously born in a single moment. The imagery signifies the rapidity of the change experienced for the people of Israel who were in exile under Babylonian rule. They will suddenly find themselves allowed to return home when Persia conquers the Babylonians. Just as the Lord would never bring a woman to the moment of giving birth and not let the child be born, so the Lord would not bring a renewed nation to the point of birth without letting the nation be born. Once the birth took place, the Lord would not close a mother's womb, a symbolic message that infers the Lord will not abandon the people of Zion after their rebirth in Zion.

The Lord invites all who love Jerusalem to rejoice. Like a mother soothing her child, the Lord will comfort, peace, satisfaction, and love. The Lord promises to "spread prosperity over her like a river," with overflowing wealth, harvest, and offspring (66:12). The heart of the Israelites shall rejoice, and their bodies shall flourish like the grass.

The Lord's power will be revealed to those who serve the Lord, and the Lord's wrath will be revealed to the Lord's enemies. Like a warrior riding on the storm winds, the Lord will come in a fiery rage and enter into judgment with fire and with the sword. The image of fire is often used in apocalyptic writings to signify the Day of Judgment. On the day the Lord comes, the Lord will slay a large multitude. Those, who have turned to idol worship by purifying themselves for worship, standing in the garden, and eating the flesh of pigs, vermin, and mice, shall come to a terrible end. All their sinful practices will end with them.

With signs and wonders, the Lord will send survivors from among the Gentiles to witness to the Lord. Nations shall flock to Jerusalem, bringing with them the relatives of the Israelites as an offering to the Lord. They shall come in a majestic procession, on horses, in chariots, in carts, on mules, and on dromedaries to Jerusalem, to the holy mountain of the Lord. The Israelites returning from exile will bring with them grain offerings for the Temple. Among the returning exiles will be priests and Levites.

The Book of Isaiah ends with an apocalyptic image of the Lord proclaiming just as the new heaven and new earth shall endure in the Lord's presence, so shall the descendants of Israel. From new moon to new moon, Sabbath to Sabbath, all will come to worship before the Lord. Those who worship will go out and view the corpses of those who rebelled against the Lord. This appears to be a reference to Gehenna outside the city where fire continued to burn and corpses were left to rot. These corpses shall be repulsive to all.

## Lectio Divina

Spend 8 to 10 minutes in silent contemplation of the following passage:

The compassionate love of the Lord reveals itself in Isaiah through the Lord's use of the image of a concerned mother who brings comfort to her children. Jesus, who is God, expresses a similar concern for Jerusalem when he proclaims over Jerusalem, "I yearned to gather your children together as a hen gathers her brood under her wings, but you were unwilling" (Luke 13:34). The Lord shows a compassionate, motherly love, for the Chosen People.

✠ *What can I learn from this passage?*

## Review Questions

1. What is the significance of nations coming to Jerusalem after the exile?
2. What does the proclamation of the Lord mean in promising that the people who harvest will eat the result of their harvest?
3. Why does the Lord need to teach the people the difference between true and false worship?

# The Book of Jeremiah (I)

### JEREMIAH 1—20

*The word of the LORD came to me: Before I formed you in the womb, I knew you, before you were born I dedicated you, a prophet to the nations I appointed you (1:4–5).*

**Opening Prayer** (SEE PAGE 16)

## Context

**Part 1: Jeremiah 1—2** The Lord had chosen Jeremiah as prophet for Judah before he was formed in the womb. He had to prophesy to a nation whose people had abandoned the Lord by worshiping the gods of foreign nations.

**Part 2: Jeremiah 3—20** The Lord is willing to receive the people back, but they remain corrupt, worshiping other gods. They are circumcised in body, but their hearts are far from the Lord of the Israelites. The people turn against Jeremiah because they refuse to believe the message of the Lord he brings to them. The Lord will punish them severely.

## PART 1: GROUP STUDY (JEREMIAH 1—2)

Read aloud Jeremiah 1—2.

### *1:1–19 The Call of Jeremiah*

The Lord's Word came to Jeremiah in the thirteenth year of the reign of Josiah, king of Judah. He prophesied during King Josiah's last years and during the reign of King Zedekiah, the son of Josiah, who reigned eleven years until the Babylonian destruction of Jerusalem in 587 BC.

Jeremiah states, "The word of the LORD came to me," a phrase often used in these prophecies to emphasize that Jeremiah is not delivering his own message, but the message of the Lord (1:2). Before his birth, the Lord dedicated and appointed him as a prophet to the nations. Jeremiah objected to the Lord's choice due to his inability to speak publicly and his youth. The Lord refuses to accept Jeremiah's objections, rejecting his claim of being too young and ordering him to speak whatever the Lord commands.

The Lord touches the mouth of Jeremiah, placing the Lord's Words in his mouth and appointing him a prophet for nations and kingdoms. Jeremiah then receives a vision. When the Lord asks Jeremiah what he sees, the prophet answers that he sees an almond tree with the blossoms appearing before its leaves burst forth. In the same way, Jeremiah's words for destroying or building will blossom before the event takes place.

In a second vision, Jeremiah describes a boiling kettle with its mouth tipped toward the south. The Lord explained the vision. Kingdoms of the north will come and surround Jerusalem and all the cities of Judah. Because the Israelites have forsaken the Lord by burning incense to other gods and paying homage to them, the Lord will bring a sentence against them.

The Lord promises to make Jeremiah as strong as a fortified city, a pillar of iron, and a wall of bronze against all of Israel. The people will fight against Jeremiah, but they will not be able to prevail, since the Lord will be with Jeremiah.

### 2:1–37 The Infidelity of Israel

The Lord directs Jeremiah to speak to the people of Jerusalem about the early days when they were devoted to the Lord like a loving bride. The Israelites were like the first fruits of a harvest, but the Lord grieved because those who plundered Israel ate of this fruit.

When the Israelites entered the Promised Land, they turned to foreign gods, an abomination before the Lord. The priests forgot about the Lord, the experts in the law did not know the Lord, the shepherds (leaders of the people) rebelled, and the prophets prophesied by Baal, a false god.

The Lord's wrath asks whether any other nation has changed gods as the people of Israel have done. They exchanged the glory of the Lord, the source of living water, for useless and weak idols that were like cisterns that crack and hold no water. The lions (Assyria and Babylon) roar against them, changing their land and cities into an uninhabited charred waste. People from Memphis, the capital of northern Egypt, and Tahpanhes, a border fortress in Egypt, shave the heads of the Israelites, humiliating them as captives. The people brought this calamity upon themselves by forsaking the Lord, the God of Israel.

The Lord asks why they go to drink the water of the Nile or to Assyrian to drink the waters of the River (a reference to the Euphrates River). The image of drinking the water of the Nile or Euphrates refers to the Israelites' worship of the gods of the nations near these waters. The Lord is asking why they are turning to an alliance with the gods of Egypt or Assyria rather than trusting in the living water and strength of the Lord.

The people of Judah rejected the Lord long ago, cutting themselves off from the Lord, living like prostitutes in serving false gods. They are like animals in heat, lusting after false gods to worship. Just as a thief is disgraced when caught, so the people of Judah—with their kings, princes, priests, and prophets—will be shamed. They will call the god made of wood their father and claim the god of stone gave them birth. They turn their back on the Lord until trouble arises, and then they cry out to the Lord.

The Lord asks sarcastically where their gods are in times of trouble. Although a woman will not forget her jewelry nor a bride her sash, yet the people forget the Lord, a much more valuable treasure. The Lord will judge the people using their own words against them. They proved themselves frivolous, choosing an alliance with Egypt against Assyria and choosing an alliance with Assyria against the northern tribes. Both nations shamed and rejected them, taking them prisoners with their hands on their heads.

## Review Questions

1. Did Jeremiah truly decide to become a prophet?
2. What reason does the Book of Jeremiah give for the destruction of Jerusalem?
3. What does the Lord mean in saying the people have become frivolous?

**Closing Prayer** (SEE PAGE 16)

Pray the closing prayer now or after *lectio divina*.

*Lectio Divina* (SEE PAGE 9)

Relax your body and maintain a posture of prayer (back straight, eyes shut, feet flat on the floor). This exercise can take as long as you want, but in the context of this Bible study, 10 to 20 minutes should be sufficient.

The meditations that follow are provided only to help group participants use this prayer form, but note that *lectio* is intended to bring one to a place of prayerful contemplation where the Word of God speaks to the hearer from his or her heart. (See page 9 for further instruction.)

## The Call of Jeremiah (1:1–19)

The Lord warns Jeremiah he will endure rejection on the part of the people in his attempt to challenge them to change their life and to listen to the Words of the Lord. Just as Jeremiah had to remain faithful to the Lord in the midst of rejection, so Christians must be willing to remain faithful to the message of the Christ when they encounter ridicule or rejection from those who refuse to follow Christ's message.

✠ *What can I learn from this passage?*

## The Infidelity of Israel (2:1–37)

For believers, the Lord is a valuable treasure touching every aspect of their life. Among those who believe are those whose faith is not strong enough to keep them from worshiping the idols of the world, such as greed, illicit pleasure, envy, sloth, and a number of other powerful temptations. Worldly desires become their treasure. Jesus knew the challenge facing all believers when he said, "For where your treasure is, there also will your heart be" (Matthew 6:21).

✠ *What can I learn from this passage?*

# PART 2: INDIVIDUAL STUDY (JEREMIAH 3—20)

## Day 1: The Consequences of Rebelling Against the Lord (3—6) *why?*

The Lord compares the Israelites to a divorced wife who becomes a prostitute with many lovers. In the Law of Moses, a divorced woman may not return to her previous husband if she marries another man after the divorce (see Deuteronomy 24:1–4). According to the Law of Moses, when Israel seeks to return to the Lord, the Lord, like a rejected husband, cannot receive her back. *huh?*

Earlier in the history of Israel, when King Solomon died, his son laid such a heavy taxation on the ten tribes of Israel in the northern area of the land that they broke away from the son of Solomon and established the northern kingdom, which became known as Israel (see 1 Kings 12:1–20). The southern kingdom, under the son of Solomon, became known as Judah. The Lord informs Jeremiah that Judah did not learn from her sister, Israel. When Israel (the northern kingdom) sinned, the Lord sent her away like a divorced wife, and she did not return. The Assyrians destroyed the northern kingdom of Israel. The people of Judah returned to the Lord after seeing what happened to Israel, but their return was not sincere. They continued to be like prostitutes by worshiping false gods.

With the destruction of the northern kingdom, the Lord spoke of the remaining people of both kingdoms as Israel. The Lord bids Israel to return to the covenant, promising not to remain angry with them. The Lord will save a remnant of the people and appoint shepherds like David, who will shepherd the people with wisdom and prudence. Jerusalem will become the Lord's throne. When the remnant returns, the remnant of the north (Israel) will settle in the southern kingdom (Judah).

In chapter 4, the Lord directs the Israelites to live with faith, working their land and fulfilling the Lord's wishes, not only by circumcising their bodies but also by circumcising their hearts. Circumcision of all male children was a sign of commitment to the covenant the Lord made with Abraham. By applying the image of circumcision to circumcising the heart, the Lord is saying that a physical fulfillment of the law does not fulfill the whole law. They must fulfill the commitment by their faithfulness to the covenant or endure the Lord's anger.

The Lord warns the cities of Judah and Jerusalem they must prepare to seek refuge against the enemy from the north, a reference to the Babylonians. The prophet urges the people to clothe themselves in sackcloth and ashes as a sign of mourning. Since they refuse to repent, the Babylonians will come upon them like a scorching wind, swifter than eagles.

Jeremiah cries out in torment over the reports of the destruction taking place. Although desolation and destruction are sweeping over the land, there are those who ignore the impending reality. They dress in fine clothing and gold, beautifying themselves. The gods, their lovers, have abandoned them. The people of Jerusalem and Judah shriek like a woman in labor in the face of those who are about to slaughter them.

In chapter 5, the Lord agrees to pardon Jerusalem if even one just person can be found. The devouring enemies—referred to as lions, wolves, and leopards—are ready to tear to pieces those who wander from their homes. The people have sinned gravely, swearing by gods who do not exist. This gives the Lord every right to punish them. Because the people rejected the Lord, a nation with a strange language will destroy them and their land.

The Lord again promises not to destroy them completely. Since the people worship foreign gods, the Lord will abandon the people to foreign rulers. Their crimes and sins have turned the Lord's blessings away from them. Criminals lurk in their midst, catching human beings instead of animals and birds in their traps. These criminals become powerful and rich, performing wicked deeds, ignoring justice, and bringing a dire judgment on orphans and the poor. Although their self-proclaimed prophets make false predictions and the priests teach on their own authority, the people accept their false words. The Lord asks the people what they will do when the end comes, implying that the prophets and priests will soon be killed and proven wrong.

In chapter 6, the Lord advises the tribes north and south of Jerusalem to prepare for the onslaught from the north. Foreign rulers and their armies, depicted by Jeremiah as evil shepherds and their flocks, will bring disaster on Zion. The enemy fearlessly invades at midday and at night.

The Lord directs Jeremiah to "glean...the remnant of Israel," to find anyone who will listen to the Word of the Lord (6:9). Like someone looking for the remainder of the grapes from the vine, the Lord is searching for any faithful followers who are left. The people lack eyes of faith, referred to as uncircumcised eyes.

The wrath of the Lord will spill over. No one will be spared, not a child, a young man, a husband, wife, or an elderly person. All have sinned in their greed, showing no shame about their wicked manner of life. The people apparently offer incense to the Lord, but as fragrant and rich as the incense is, their incense and sacrifices find no favor with the Lord. The Babylonians will come on their horses, sounding like the roaring sea and carrying their weapons ready for a merciless slaughter. When the people of Judah hear them coming, they will stand helpless before them, writhing in anguish like a woman in labor. The Israelites shall be called "Silver rejected," because they failed the test of trusting in the Lord.

### Lectio Divina

*never heard that before*

Spend 8 to 10 minutes in silent contemplation of the following passage:

Because our life seems so endless, we may tend to be more concerned about the present than we are about our eternal destiny. Although the Israelites knew the Babylonians were drawing closer to their land, they thought only of their present luxurious state of life. Our life will end just as their life had to end, but they were not preparing for it. Jesus tells us we must always be prepared.

✠ *What can I learn from this passage?*

## Day 2: Jeremiah's Temple Discourse (7—10)

Jeremiah exhorts the people to reform their life so the Lord may dwell with them in the Temple. Although the people believe the presence of the Temple in the land will save them, Jeremiah declares believing the Temple will save them is not true. They must change their ways of treating their neighbor, not oppressing the orphan, the widow, not killing the innocent, or worshiping false gods. Only if the people follow the ways of the Lord will the Lord continue to dwell in the Temple and in the land the Lord gave their ancestors long ago.

The Lord challenges the people to look honestly at themselves. Do they really think they can steal, murder, commit adultery, swear falsely, sacrifice to Baal, worship other unknown gods, and then come to the Temple to worship the Lord? The people have made the Temple a den of thieves.

The Lord directs the people to look to Shiloh, an important shrine that once housed the Ark of the Covenant before the Ark was moved to the Temple in Jerusalem. Because of the sinfulness of the priests serving in the sanctuary at Shiloh, the Lord allowed the Philistines to destroy Shiloh and capture the Ark (see 1 Samuel 4:1–11). Just as the Lord allowed the sanctuary at Shiloh to be destroyed because of the sinfulness of the people, so the Lord will do the same to the Temple in Jerusalem due to the sins of the people.

The Lord tells Jeremiah to witness to the sinfulness of the people. Families sin when they make cakes for the "queen of heaven," a reference to Astarte, the false goddess of fertility, and when they make offerings to other gods. The people remain stubborn, turning their backs on the Lord and living in sin. From the day the people left Egypt to the time of Jeremiah, the Lord sent servants, the prophets, to the people, but they did not listen and became greater sinners than their ancestors.

The Lord, warning Jeremiah the people will not listen to him, tells him to confront the people with the truth about their unfaithfulness. The Lord directs Jeremiah to cut off his hair and throw it away as a sign of mourning.

Areas around Jerusalem were used to sacrificing the people's sons and daughters to the gods, and now these forms of worship have come into the Temple. Topheth, one of the places of such horrible worship, will become a burial ground for the overwhelming number of corpses during the Babylonian invasion. Some will not be buried and become food for the birds and animals.

In chapter 8, the Lord relates a further abomination by the leaders of the people. Instead of treating the corpses of the kings, princes, priests, prophets, and inhabitants of Jerusalem with the usual respect for the dead, their bones will be taken from their graves and spread out before the sun, moon, and hosts of heaven that they loved and worshiped as gods.

The Lord wonders why the people never learn their lesson. When people fall, they rise again, and when they turn away, they turn back. They keep headlong on the same path like a horse rushing into battle. The stork, turtledove, swallow, and crane know the seasons and the time of their return. The people, however, do not know the law of the Lord, and they follow the lying words of any scribe who teaches them. The wise have rejected the Word of the Lord and have no wisdom to share. The Lord will punish them by giving their wives to other men, their fields to new owners. The prophets and priests speak of peace with no peace to share. They shall be punished.

When the people entered the Promised Land, the Lord gave them an abundance of grapes and figs, but now there are none. Because they sinned, the Lord gave them poisoned water to drink. From the north comes the sound of horses shaking the land, coming to devastate the land and its inhabitants. Tears have replaced joy in the hearts of those who ask if the Lord of Zion has abandoned them. Jeremiah asks if there is no balm in Gilead, an area south of the Sea of Galilee known for its healing balm, since all healing has ended in Jerusalem.

The speaker wishes to find "a travelers' lodging" in the wilderness, an escape from the adulterous people who are betraying the Lord (9:1). The Lord warns the people not to trust their deceiving neighbors, namely other nations. These neighbors speak of peace, but in their hearts they are planning a snare for the people.

The Lord wails over the mountains and the scorched pastures of Judah that have become such a wasteland, even the birds and beasts have fled. In ancient times, women would come and mourn when someone died, causing others to mourn. The Lord asks for women who are skilled at mourning to come and lament in such a manner that the people will weep bitterly. The devastation shall be immense, with death for young and old everywhere in the city. Corpses will be as massive as dung in an open field, like sheaves behind the reaper with no one to gather them.

The Lord will soon demand an account of all those who are circumcised. The men of other nations are not circumcised as the people of Judah, but the Lord knows many of the people of Judah are uncircumcised at heart. They do not live up to the covenant commitment that is meant to accompany physical circumcision.

In chapter 10, Jeremiah continues to proclaim the message he received from the Lord, reminding the Israelites that the idols the nations worship are simply creations of their own imagination. They are like scarecrows in a field who cannot speak. They are the creation of hammer and nails, needing to be carried because they cannot walk.

Jeremiah praises the power of the Lord and declares no one is like the Lord. The idols are mere silver and gold from the coastlands, the work of skilled artisans. The true God is the living God of Israel whose wrath the nations cannot tolerate. The true skilled artisan is the Lord, who created the earth, the heavens, lightning and rain, and the wind. The worshipers of idols are too stupid to know the Lord, so they bow down before false idols that will perish.

In verse 17, the land of Zion becomes the speaker, urging the people to flee from the land. The city laments that the wounds of the city will not be healed. At an earlier time, the people of Zion refused to admit the siege, referred to as the sickness of the city, would end with the total destruction of the city. The word in Zion is a movement from the north will make the cities of Judah a wasteland.

In verse 25, Jeremiah again speaks. He admits the people's need for correction but begs the Lord to act with fairness, not with an angry fury that would lead to annihilation for the nation. He pleads for punishment on the nations who do not know the Lord and have destroyed the land of Israel.

### Lectio Divina

Spend 8 to 10 minutes in silent contemplation of the following passage:

Despite the sinfulness of the Israelites, they pray with the hope the compassionate God will forgive their sins and protect them. Jeremiah continually calls the people to repent so the Lord can forgive them. Throughout the Gospels, Jesus reveals an image of a compassionate God anxious to forgive the sins of those who truly seek forgiveness and who strive to remain faithful to the Lord. The Scriptures offer hope to sinners.

✠ *What can I learn from this passage?*

## Day 3: Plots Against Jeremiah (11—14)

The Lord speaks to Jeremiah about fidelity to the covenant. If the Israelites remain faithful to the covenant, then the Lord would be their God, and they would belong to him. When the Israelites left Egypt under Moses' leadership, the Lord promised to lead them to a land flowing with milk and honey. Jeremiah answers, "Amen," agreeing the Lord's part in the covenant has been fulfilled. From the time the Lord brought the Israelites out of Egypt to the present, the Lord warned the people about remaining faithful to the covenant, but they stubbornly refused. As a result, the Lord will bring about a devastation they cannot escape.

The Israelites' false gods have become as numerous as the cities of Judah and the altars of sacrifice to Baal have become as numerous as the streets of Jerusalem. The Lord directs Jeremiah not to intercede for the people.

In a short canticle in chapter 11, the Lord speaks to Zion, asking what right a beloved (Zion) has in the house of the Lord while living sinfully. The people continue to offer worship to the Lord, but the Lord asks if they expect these external actions to free them from the impending disaster. The Lord once referred to Israel as a spreading olive tree, producing good fruit, but now the Lord will devour them in flames because of the evil Israel and Judah chose in sacrificing to Baal.

Verse 18 begins one of several laments attributed to Jeremiah. Jeremiah asserts he is being led to the slaughter like an innocent, trusting lamb, unaware that some false prophets were plotting against him. Their intent is to kill Jeremiah while he was still young (a tree in its vigor). Jeremiah pleads with the Lord to allow him to witness the Lord's vengeance on them.

In verse 21, the Lord speaks to Jeremiah concerning people from a town named Anathoth, Jeremiah's birthplace, who wanted to kill him. In response to the threat against Jeremiah, the Lord plans to annihilate the people of Anathoth, killing their young men by the sword and their offspring by famine.

In chapter 12, Jeremiah complains to the Lord, laying out his case as though he were in court. He asks why the wicked flourish and urges the Lord to select the evil ones as sheep for the slaughter. He asks how long the land must mourn because of the wickedness of those who dwell there and who say the Lord does not care about their actions.

The Lord responds, asking Jeremiah if running against men has wearied him. What will happen to him when he races against horses? In other words, if Jeremiah has become weary with all that has happened so far, what will he do when his situation becomes worse and more challenging?

Jeremiah's anguish will increase when his own relatives betray him and enlist a force against him.

The Lord laments the punishment endured by the people of Judah. The Lord's heritage (Judah) has become like a victim in the forest, deserving the Lord's hatred, living as prey for hyenas, vultures, and wild animals who come and devour her. Many of Jerusalem's leaders (shepherds) have ravaged and crushed Jerusalem and turned it into a wasteland where looters dwell. The people planted wheat and reaped thorns, meaning the people lived well when they entered the land given to them by the Lord, but they became idol worshipers. Instead of harvesting peace, they harvested the burning wrath of the Lord.

The Lord will turn Israel and Judah over to the plunderers. After taking them from the land, the Lord will have compassion on them and bring each one back to the land. If the plunderers learn to swear by the name of the Lord of Israel just as they taught the Lord's people to swear by Baal, then they shall flourish in the midst of the Israelites. If they do not learn to obey the Lord, the Lord will destroy that nation.

In chapter 13, the Lord directs Jeremiah to perform the first of several symbolic acts. He is to purchase a loincloth and wear it on his loins. After Jeremiah bought the loincloth and put it on, the Lord spoke to him a second time, telling him to take the loincloth that he is wearing and go to the Euphrates (Perath) where he is to hide it in the cleft of a rock. Jeremiah did as the Lord directed. After a long period, the Lord directed Jeremiah to go to Perath and fetch the loincloth, which he did, and found it was rotten and good for nothing.

The Lord draws a lesson from the symbolic action of the loincloth. In the same way the loincloth rotted, so the Lord will allow Judah to rot since the people disobeyed the Lord and worshiped false gods. Just as a loincloth clings to a man's loins, so the Lord decreed the people of Israel and Judah should cling to the Lord of Israel who called them to be the Lord's people. The people, however, did not heed the Lord.

In the same manner, the Lord will make everyone in the land drunk with the wrath of the Lord. The Lord will then smash the people, one against another, causing havoc in the land. The Lord will show no compassion or pity but will destroy them all.

The Lord instructs the people not to be arrogant. They are to glorify the Lord, their God, lest the Lord casts darkness upon them. They will stumble, light will turn to darkness, and black clouds will cover them. If the people do not listen, the Lord will weep copious tears in secret for the Lord's flock led into exile.

Jeremiah is to tell the king and the mother of the king to descend from their throne. They will no longer wear the crown, and the cities of Negeb (the southern territory of Judah) will be under siege with no one to defend them. All of Judah will be taken into exile.

The Lord calls upon Judah to look at the invaders coming from the north. What will the nation of Judah say when the invaders, whom they thought were their allies, set up rulers over the land of Judah? Judah will experience pain like a woman in labor and the Israelites will ask why this is happening to them. The ravaging of the land will be like the raping of a woman whose skirts are stripped away. The Lord declares Judah will find it as difficult to turn to goodness as it is for Ethiopians to change their skin or leopards to change their spots. The Lord will scatter the Israelites like chaff in the wind. Because the people forgot the Lord, the Lord will bring them shame.

In chapter 14, the Lord speaks to Jeremiah concerning a drought in the land. The waterless soil is ruined, the doe deserts her young, and wild donkeys gasp for breath growing weaker from lack of grass. In desperation, the people ask why the Lord should act like a stranger in the land, unable to act like a conqueror. The Lord, however, does not believe the people are capable of changing. Because of the guilt of the people, the Lord takes no delight in them and will punish them. The Lord, instructing Jeremiah not to intercede for the people, refuses to listen to their fasting, sacrifices, burnt offerings, or grain offerings and plans to destroy them with the sword, famine, and plague.

Jeremiah reports the prophets say the people will not experience the sword or famine, and they prophesy the Lord promised lasting peace for Judah. The Lord denies speaking to these prophets. They are prophesying false visions, idiotic divinations, and deceptions that originate in their own imagination. The false prophets who prophesy in the Lord's name, although the Lord did not send them, will experience the sword and famine. The people who accepted their prophecies will experience the same punishment. As a result of their wickedness, no one will bury them.

The Lord tells Jeremiah to deliver his (Jeremiah's) lament to the people. Jeremiah declares his eyes stream with tears day and night over the immense destruction of Jerusalem. He laments over a wound that was unable to be healed. In the field, he encounters those slain by the sword, and in the city the Lord encounters the victims of famine. The prophet and priest fruitlessly attempt to fulfill their roles in a land they no longer recognize.

In verse 19, the people speak. They ask why the Lord has struck them with a punishment that cannot heal. They wait in vain for peace and encounter terror instead. They admit their sinfulness and the sins of their ancestors, begging the Lord, for the Lord's own sake, not to reject them and bring disgrace on the name of the Lord. The people challenge the Lord not to break the covenant with them, finally admitting the Lord alone and not the gods of the nations can produce rain.

### Lectio Divina

Spend 8 to 10 minutes in silent contemplation of the following passage:

Just as Jeremiah wept over the destruction of Jerusalem, so Jesus did the same. In the Gospel of Luke, Jesus weeps over Jerusalem, predicting the enemy will smash the city and the children in it to the ground and not leave one stone upon another (see Luke 19:41–44). The people of Jesus' day refused to recognize the presence of the Lord in their midst, just as the people of Israel refused to listen to the warning given by the Lord. The concern of Jeremiah and Jesus reflects the loving compassion of God.

✠ *What can I learn from this passage?*

## Day 4: The Lord's Unchangeable Verdict (15—17)

The Lord firmly refuses to reconsider the punishment inflicted on the people. Even if Moses and Samuel stood before the Lord, the Lord would not withdraw the judgment cast on the people. The Lord has decreed four types of scourges against the people. The sword will kill them, dogs will drag them off, the birds and beasts will devour them, and they will be an object of horror to all the nations because of the sins of Manasseh, son of Hezekiah, king of Judah. King Manasseh practiced abominations and evils greater than all those before him (see 2 Kings 21:9–16).

The Lord allowed the enemy to destroy Jerusalem with the hope the people would repent, but they refused to turn away from their sins. The number of widows increased with the death of the men. The mother of seven, who would ordinarily be considered favored by the Lord, will faint at the death of her sons.

Jeremiah laments, addressing Jerusalem as his mother and regretting the day he was born. The controversy he endures does not come from the ordinary conflicts of lending or borrowing but from his service to the Lord. Despite his prayers, Jeremiah recognizes the weakness of the people of Judah against the iron or bronze weapons of the Babylonians. The Lord's fiery wrath will allow the enemy to plunder Judah and lead the people as slaves to a strange land.

Jeremiah asks the Lord to take vengeance on his persecutors. For the Lord's sake, he has accepted insults. The mood momentarily changes as Jeremiah admits finding joy and happiness in the Words of the Lord, which he devours. He, however, has no time for celebrating but becomes enraged under the burden placed on him by the Lord. Jeremiah claims his wound refuses to be healed, and he dares to speak of the Lord as a deceptive brook whose waters sometimes fail.

The Lord responds to Jeremiah's plight as though Jeremiah were resigning from his role as a prophet. The Lord calls him back into service, allowing him to continue to stand in the Lord's presence and act as the Lord's mouthpiece. The people will come to Jeremiah instead of Jeremiah going to them, and the Lord will protect him as though he were a wall of bronze. Those who fight against him will fail because the Lord will rescue him from the hand of the wicked and violent.

In chapter 16, the Lord directs Jeremiah not to marry to avoid having sons and daughters in Judah. The land will be devastated by a deadly disease, with corpses lying everywhere for the birds and wild animals to eat. Those who do not die will be killed by the sword or famine. The loss of compassion on the part of the Lord continues as the Lord directs Jeremiah not to enter a house of mourning to grieve for the deceased. Because of the

*Too many dead to mourn each one*

number of the dead, the people will omit the usual ceremonies of mourning, such as gashing themselves or shaving one's head, or sharing consolation with those mourning, such as sharing food or drink.

*punished for sins part of present*

The Lord tells Jeremiah not to enter a house for feasting or drinking with the people because the Lord will silence the song of joy and gladness, and the song of the bridegroom and bride. When the people ask Jeremiah why the Lord is punishing them, he answers it is due to the sins of their ancestors who turned away from the Lord to follow other gods. It is also due to the far worse sins of the present generations who stubbornly refuse to listen to the Lord.

A later editor inserted a short passage in verses 14 and 15 concerning the end of the exile that took place many decades after Jeremiah. The days will come when people will no longer speak of the Lord leading the Israelites out of Egypt, but people will speak of the Lord bringing the people out of the north (Babylon) and out of the other countries into which the Lord banished them. The Lord will bring them back to the land the Lord gave their ancestors.

Using an image of fishermen sent out to catch sinners who are in exile and an image of a hunter sent out to hunt all those who believe they are hidden from the Lord, the Lord declares no one can remain hidden. The Lord will punish the oppressors of the Israelites with double punishment for profaning the land of Judah with the carcasses of their detestable idols and abominations. After the exile, nations will come streaming to the Lord from the ends of the earth and say their ancestors inherited empty idols that human beings made for themselves as gods. These nations will acknowledge the Lord of Jeremiah is the Lord over all.

Chapter 17 speaks of the sin of Judah being engraved with an iron stylus or diamond point in the hearts of the people of Judah, never to be erased. The Lord will turn the treasures of Judah over to plunder as payment for their sins, and they will lose the heritage they received from the Lord. The Lord curses those who trust in human beings more than the Lord and blesses those who remain faithful to the covenant, likening them to a tree "that stretches out its roots to the stream" (17:8).

The Lord asks who can understand the human heart. The reference is obviously to the symbolic use of the word heart, which refers to one's desire for good or evil. The Lord explores the mind of human beings and tests the heart, giving to all what they deserve. Using the image of a partridge, which hatches the eggs it did not lay, the Lord warns those who acquire wealth unjustly they will be seen as fools when their wealth eludes them in midlife.

Jeremiah speaks of the Lord as a throne of glory, exalted from the beginning, the hope of Israel. Those who forsake the Lord will be disgraced and enrolled in the underworld because they have forsaken the source of living water. The people ridicule him, challenging him to show the fulfillment of the Word of the Lord. Jeremiah prays the Lord will become a refuge for him, confounding his persecutors but not persecuting him. Jeremiah asks the Lord to double the destruction in store for them.

The Lord instructs Jeremiah to warn the people not to carry goods on the Sabbath by bringing them in through the gates of Jerusalem. In the Book of Nehemiah, the author speaks of foreigners importing every type of merchandise into Jerusalem on the Sabbath. Reminding the people the Lord punished their ancestors for working on the Sabbath, Nehemiah orders the gates of Jerusalem to be closed on the Sabbath (see Nehemiah 13:15–22). The people are to refrain from all work on the Sabbath as the Lord commanded their ancestors.

If the people obey the law, making the Sabbath a day of rest and abstaining from all work, then the kings who sit on the throne of David and all the inhabitants will continue to enter the city of Jerusalem. People will come from the cities of Judah (Benjamin, Shephelah, and Negeb) and bring their animals, grain offerings, and incense to the Temple. If the people do keep holy the Sabbath, then the Lord will set fire to the gates and destroy Jerusalem.

### Lectio Divina

Spend 8 to 10 minutes in silent contemplation of the following passage:

A man told his pastor he was always afraid to abandon himself totally to the will of God. He feared the Lord would respond by testing him with some unbearable sickness or emotional affliction. In a similar fashion, the Lord asked for trust from the Israelites, but many of them had difficulty believing the Lord would free them from the onslaught of the enemy. Trusting the Lord in every aspect of our life involves intense faith and love of God.

✠ *What can I learn from this passage?*

## Day 5: The Potter's Vessel (18—20)

The Lord directs Jeremiah to go to a potter's house where the Lord will speak to him. At the potter's house, Jeremiah notes that the potter, when the vessel of clay he was shaping was not pleasing, remade it until it pleased him. Since Israel was like clay in the hand of the Lord, the Lord asks Jeremiah why the Lord could not do to Israel what the potter had done to the clay. The Lord may decree destruction of a people or nation for its evil ways, but if the nation turns away from its evil, then the Lord will have a change of heart. In the same manner, the Lord may decree prosperity for a nation or kingdom, but if the nation does what is evil, then the Lord will have a change of heart concerning the blessings the Lord planned for that nation.

When the people of Israel turn away from the Lord of Israel, nations will witness the destruction taking place in Israel. It will be as permanent as the snow of Lebanon, a reference to a mountain peak in Lebanon that is always covered with snow. It will be as permanent as the water rushing down the mountains. The Israelites have forgotten their Lord, offering incense to nothing, not following the path of the Lord, the track laid out by the Lord. The devastation of the land shall become such a waste, those passing by would hiss at it. Hissing was a practice of pagan worshipers to ward off evil demons they believed dwelt in the land.

When the Israelites hear the words of their priests, wise men, and prophets who prophesy good things for the people, the people believe them and plot against Jeremiah. Jeremiah calls upon the Lord to curse them, reminding the Lord he once spoke in favor of them to avert the Lord's anger against them. Now he calls upon the Lord to afflict their children with famine, to kill them with the sword, to make their wives childless and widows, to send a plague on their husbands, and to slaughter their youth with the sword. He reminds the Lord they dug a pit and hid traps to capture him, planning to kill him. He prays the Lord will not forgive or forget their crime.

The Lord directs Jeremiah to buy a potter's earthenware flask and, with some of the elders and priests, to go to the entrance of the Potsherd Gate, which was on the south wall of Jerusalem where dung and other trash were pitched into the Valley of Ben-hinnom. There, Jeremiah was to deliver the Word of the Lord concerning the destruction of the people of Judah and Jerusalem. They burnt incense to false gods unknown to the ancestors, and their kings built sanctuaries to sacrifice as an offering to Baal the innocent blood of children, an action the Lord would never command them to do.

The Lord warns the days are coming when the place for slaughtering children for Baal shall no longer be called Topheth, in the Valley of Ben-hinnom, but rather the Valley of Slaughter. The Lord will allow the inhabitants of Judah and Jerusalem to be slaughtered and their corpses eaten by the birds and beasts. The city will become a waste and an object of hissing by those who pass by. As a result of the miseries of the Babylonian invasion, the people will turn to cannibalism.

After Jeremiah preached these words, the Lord directed him to break the potter's flask and declare the Lord will smash the people and the city to the point where no one can repair it. Topheth, the place of slaughter, will become the burial place of many of the people. The houses of the king of Judah and people of Jerusalem will be defiled as dreadful as the place of Topheth.

In chapter 20, a priest name Pashhur, who was the chief officer of the Temple, heard Jeremiah's words and, striking him, put him in stocks at the upper Gate of Benjamin in the Temple. The next morning, when Pashhur released Jeremiah, Jeremiah prophesied the Lord would change the name of Pashhur to "Terror on every side," because of the terror he shall experience when the Lord turns him and his friends over to the Babylonians. Because Pashhur prophesied lies, he and his family will go into exile in Babylon where Pashhur will be buried along with his friends.

Jeremiah's frustration as a prophet leads him to complain. He claims the Lord deceived him, and he admits his greatest frustration is he allowed the Lord to deceive him. Because the Lord overpowered him, seducing him to accept the role of a prophet in Judah, people mock and ridicule him for the message he brings, a message of violence and outrage. He declares he will not mention or speak in the name of the Lord again, but he cannot hold back the Word of the Lord, which is like a burning fire in his heart. He hears people who were his friends whispering and plotting to make any misstep a reason to take revenge on him.

Jeremiah suddenly becomes more courageous, declaring his trust in the Lord. The Lord will make his persecutors fail and experience unforgettable disgrace. Jeremiah pleads with the Lord to allow him to see the vengeance the Lord casts upon the enemy.

In another turn of emotion, Jeremiah curses the day he was born. He harshly curses the messenger who brought to his father the news that he had a son. If he had been killed in the womb, his mother's womb would have been his grave and he would not have experienced the sight of sorrow and pain, which, he believes, will bring him shame to the end of his days.

### Lectio Divina

Spend 8 to 10 minutes in silent contemplation of the following passage:

When Jeremiah experienced rejection from those closest to him, he complained to the Lord and became deeply depressed. Since the people kept rejecting his message, he wondered about the value of his life. The message for us is we also may feel the absence of God, but we must recognize it as a step in our spiritual growth, an empty time when the Lord is challenging us to show a deeper faith and love.

✠ *What can I learn from this passage?*

## Review Questions

1. What does the Lord wish to receive from the people in order to deliver them from their enemies?
2. What made the people believe they would not face destruction because of the presence of the Temple and the land?
3. Why does the Lord forbid Jeremiah to lament or grieve for the many who have died by the sword, famine, or plague?
4. What is the message of the potter's vessel?

## LESSON 6

# The Book of Jeremiah (II)

### JEREMIAH 21—35

*See, days are coming—oracle of the LORD—when I will raise up a righteous branch for David; As king he shall reign and govern wisely, he shall do what is just and right in the land (23:5).*

**Opening Prayer** (SEE PAGE 16)

## Context

**Part 1: Jeremiah 21—23:8** Jeremiah declares the Lord will fight against the people of Judah. The Lord casts woes on the kings of Judah and concludes by promising days are coming when the Lord will raise up a just king for the people.

**Part 2: Jeremiah 23:9—35:19** Jeremiah predicts seventy years of exile for the people, and endures the threat of death for his prophecies. The Lord instructs the people of Judah to serve the king of Babylon or perish. When the people go into exile in Babylon, Jeremiah sends a letter to them, directing them to live a normal life in exile, building homes and marrying, promising the day will come when Judah shall be restored. When the king of Babylon conquers the people of Judah, King Zedekiah of Judah and all his princes will be handed over to the king of Babylon.

# PART 1: GROUP STUDY (JEREMIAH 21—23:8)

Read aloud Jeremiah 21—23:8.

### *21:1–14 The Fate of Zedekiah*

Zedekiah, the king of Judah, rebelled against the king of Babylon, who retaliated by laying siege to the city and destroying it in 587 BC. King Nebuchadnezzar of Babylon captured Zedekiah as he attempted to flee, put out his eyes, shackled him, and led him off into exile in Babylon. The Babylonians destroyed all of Jerusalem by fire (see 2 Kings 25:1–12). At the time the rebellion of Zedekiah began, the king sent a man named Pash-hur (not the same Pashhur mentioned in Jeremiah 20:1–6) and a priest named Zephaniah to Jeremiah to speak to the Lord for them, believing that the Lord who had preserved the nation in the past would do the same at this time.

Jeremiah prophesied that the Lord would turn against Zedekiah's kingdom, killing the people and beasts of Jerusalem. The Book of 2 Kings states Zedekiah did what was evil in the sight of the Lord (see 2 Kings 24:19–20). The Lord will bring plague, famine, and death upon the city and hand over Zedekiah, his ministers and the survivors of the siege to Nebuchadnezzar. The survivors will have a choice of remaining in the city and being slaughtered or surrendering themselves to Nebuchadnezzar who will allow them to live in exile.

The Lord addresses Jerusalem as a "Ruler of the Valley, Rock of the Plains," which is a reference to the natural fortification of the city built on a mountain. The Lord pledges to punish Jerusalem with fire in the forest, an apparent reference to the palace of the king that was named "the House of the Forest of Lebanon" during the time of Solomon, since it was built of cedar (see 1 Kings 7:2).

### *22:1—23:8 The Fate of the Kings*

The Lord sends Jeremiah to warn the king, his ministers, and all the people who enter the holy city to rescue victims from their oppressors. They are to avoid wronging foreigners, orphans, and widows and "not shed innocent blood" (22:3). Despite the beauty and grandeur of Jerusalem's palaces, which were built with cedar wood from the forests of Gilead and Lebanon, the Lord will "cut down" these "choice cedars" (22:7). Passersby will ask why the Lord has done this, and the answer they will receive is the people of Judah abandoned the covenant with the Lord their God by worshiping and serving false gods. The Lord tells the people not to weep for the dead but for those who are led away from the land never to return.

The Lord condemns Jehoiakim, king of Judah, who, forcing his neighbors to work without pay, constructs a luxurious house. He builds a palace with many well-aired rooms, with windows, cedar panels, and walls painted bright red. The Lord reminds him his father prospered, eating and drinking well because he acted with justice for the weak and poor. Jehoiakim, on the other hand, set his eyes and heart on personal gain, shedding innocent blood and oppressing the people. Because Jehoiakim acted unjustly, no one shall lament him. He shall be buried like a donkey, cast outside the gate. A donkey was ordinarily not buried but dumped outside of Jerusalem. According to 2 Kings, however, Jehoiakim was buried among his ancestors (see 2 Kings 24:6).

Addressing the city as though it were a person, the Lord bids Jerusalem to climb to the high mountains surrounding her and see that all her lovers are destroyed. The lovers represent the nations that once defended Jerusalem. The wind will shepherd their shepherds, meaning their shepherds—the leaders—shall become as weak as rubble in the wind, and their lovers shall go into exile.

The Lord says if King Coniah of Judah were a signet ring on the Lord's right hand, the Lord would snatch it off. Coniah is an abbreviated name for Jeconiah. Rulers wore signet rings continually on their right hands and would use the symbol on the ring to seal letters. In the gesture of tearing off the ring, the Lord is totally rejecting Jeconiah. The Lord will turn him over to Nebuchadnezzar, king of Babylon. The Lord will cast Jeconiah and his mother out to a land that they never knew, never to return. Since all of King Coniah's children will die, he will be considered childless, a curse in Israel.

The Lord will punish the current leaders (shepherds) for not caring for the people of Judah and driving them away. The Lord promises to gather a remnant from the lands to which the Lord banished them and place over them shepherds who will lead them with justice rather than fear. Some day the Lord will "raise up a righteous branch for David" (23:5). During his reign, the Lord will save Judah and bring security to Israel. The name of the new ruler will be "the LORD our justice" (23:6).

The return of the exiles from Babylon shall take the place of the Exodus in the minds of the people, as they recall the time the Lord freed them. The Lord will call people from all nations to which they have been banished, and they shall live on their own soil.

## Review Questions

1. Why did Zedekiah and the people of Jerusalem keep ignoring the prophecies of Jeremiah?
2. What does Jeremiah mean when he claims the Lord tells Coniah that even if he were a signet ring on the Lord's right hand, the Lord will still hand him over to the king of Babylon?
3. Who are the shepherds found in the Book of Jeremiah who destroy and scatter the flock?

---

**Closing Prayer** (SEE PAGE 16)

Pray the closing prayer now or after *lectio divina*.

---

**Lectio Divina** (SEE PAGE 9)

Relax your body and maintain a posture of prayer (back straight, eyes shut, feet flat on the floor). This exercise can take as long as you want, but in the context of this Bible study, 10 to 20 minutes should be sufficient.

The meditations that follow are provided only to help group participants use this prayer form, but note that *lectio* is intended to bring one to a place of prayerful contemplation where the Word of God speaks to the hearer from his or her heart. (See page 9 for further instruction.)

### The Fate of Zedekiah (21:1–14)

The fate of Zedekiah illustrates the Lord's anger when those chosen to shepherd the people reject the Lord and rule unjustly. Parents are the shepherds of their children both physically and spiritually. Pastors, teachers, doctors, nurses, civic leaders, and all who serve others or have authority over others are shepherds, physically as well as spiritually. Unfortunately, rulers and others in authority have a greater concern for the physical well-being of those they serve while neglecting their spiritual well-being. We can learn a lesson from the story of King Zedekiah.

✠ *What can I learn from this passage?*

### The Fate of the Kings (22:1—23:8)

Despite the sinfulness of the Israelites, the Lord promises a just leader will return to rebuild the city of David. During Advent, the Catholic Church prepares to celebrate the birth of Jesus, the "righteous shoot" and "branch" that fulfills many Old Testament prophecies. In the annunciation, the angel Gabriel announces to Mary that "the Lord God will give him the throne of David his father" (Luke 1:32). This new king will usher in a new era, not just for the Israelites but for all creation.

✠ *What can I learn from this passage?*

# PART 2: INDIVIDUAL STUDY (JEREMIAH 23:9—35:19)

## Day 1: Just Shepherds and False Prophets (23:9—25:38)

Jeremiah laments over the people who are worshiping false gods while the land withers away, the powerful lead unjustly, and the prophets and priests are godless. Because of the wickedness of the leaders, the Lord will bring disaster upon them. The prophets of Samaria shocked the Lord by worshiping Baal and leading the people astray. Looking to the prophets of Jerusalem, the Lord witnessed something more shocking, namely, adultery (worshiping and serving false gods), deception, and the power of the wicked that hinders people from turning away from evil. The evil of the people becomes so great it is like the cities of Sodom and Gomorrah, which were destroyed because of their incredible sinfulness.

The Lord tells the people not to listen to the empty words of the prophets whose words do not come from the Lord but from their own imagination. They proclaim peace and declare the people will not experience evil. In doing this, they are rejecting the Word of the Lord. The wrath of the Lord against these prophets shall be like a raging storm and not subside until they are punished. In the days ahead, the people of Judah will understand the Lord did not send these prophets despite their prophecies. The Lord questions whether those who prophesy lies and deceptions will ever turn back to the Lord. Using a proverb, the Lord contrasts straw (false prophets) with wheat (true prophets). The true Word of the Lord is like fire or like a hammer that shatters rock. When the people, prophets, or priests ask Jeremiah to identify the burden of the Lord, he answers they are the burden of the Lord.

The message of chapter 24 takes place after the Babylonians have invaded the land of Judah and sent King Jehoiakim of Judah, the princes of Judah, and the skilled workers into exile in Babylon. The Lord places two baskets of figs in front of the Temple of the Lord. One basket contains ripe figs and the other rotten figs. When the Lord asks Jeremiah what he sees, the prophet declares he sees good figs and bad figs. The Lord likens the good figs to the exiles who the Lord will favor. The Lord promises to protect them and bring them back to the land "to build them up, not tear them down; to plant them, not uproot them" (24:6). The Lord will bless them with a heart to know their Lord is truly Lord. "They shall be my people and I will be their God," the Lord says, "for they shall return to me with their whole heart" (24:7).

The attention of the Lord turns to the bad figs that cannot be eaten. The Lord will make Zedekiah, the king of Judah, his princes, the remnant of Jerusalem who remains in the land, and those who settled in Egypt like the bad figs, objects of horror to all the kingdoms of the world. The Lord will punish them with the sword, famine, and plague until they pass into oblivion.

In chapter 25, Jeremiah predicts for the first time the length of the exile inflicted on the people of Judah by the Babylonians. He dates his prophecy as taking place in the fourth year of the reign of Jehoiakim, king of Judah, at the time Nebuchadnezzar became king of Babylon. For twenty-three years, Jeremiah and other prophets of the Lord warned the people of Judah, but they refused to listen. The Lord warned the people not to turn to evil and worship other gods, but they would not listen to the Words of the Lord. As a result, the Lord will send Nebuchadnezzar upon them and all neighboring nations.

Jeremiah refers to Nebuchadnezzar as the Lord's servant, showing the destruction of Judah is an act of God. The destruction shall be so great the land and its inhabitants will be objects of horror and hissing. Darkness will pervade. After seventy years, the Lord will punish the king of Babylon and the land of the Chaldeans for their sins. Their land will become desolate. Those inhabitants, whose deeds were wicked, will receive a wicked end, serving as slaves in other nations under other kings.

The Lord presents a cup of the wine of wrath to Jeremiah and directs him to have all the nations to whom the Lord sends him drink from the cup. The Lord predicts they will drink it, vomit, and go insane because of the sword the Lord will set upon them. Jeremiah takes the cup and gives it to the nations, beginning in Jerusalem, the cities of Judah, and all the nations surrounding Judah. Even if the nations refuse to drink from the cup, they will still drink of the Lord's wrath. Nation after nation shall encounter the devastation of the sword. Like a violent storm that erupts from the depths of the earth, the wrath of the Lord will roar over all the nations.

Jeremiah announces bodies will cover the earth. Since all people must fend for themselves, no one will mourn or bury the corpses, which will lie like dung on the ground. The shepherds (leaders of the people) shall wail and flounder about, knowing the time for their slaughter has arrived. Like a lion that leaves its lair, the wrath of the Lord brings desolation to the land and death by the sword to many.

### Lectio Divina

Spend 8 to 10 minutes in silent contemplation of the following passage:

The false prophets refused to listen to the Lord's predictions as given to Jeremiah, and they falsely spoke of the Lord blessing and saving the people. In the end, they suffered along with the people. The Lord calls us to a life of loving one another, but in the process, we must remain faithful to our covenant and trust in the Lord, especially in difficult times.

✠ *What can I learn from this passage?*

## Day 2: Jeremiah Threatened With Death (26—27)

Hoping the people will listen and turn from their evil ways, the Lord sends Jeremiah to the Temple to speak again to the people. When the priests, prophets, and people hear Jeremiah's words, they seize him, believing he was degrading the Temple by declaring it will become like Shiloh and the city of Jerusalem shall become uninhabited. Jeremiah's accusers believe the Temple, the house of the Lord, and the city of David would last forever. They bring Jeremiah before the princes to demand he be put to death because of his blasphemy.

Jeremiah states the Lord sent him to prophesy against the Temple and the city. He entreats the people to reform their lives and to listen to the voice of the Lord. Jeremiah was willing to accept their verdict against him, adding that in killing him, they are taking his innocent blood on themselves, the city, and its inhabitants.

The princes and all the people tell the priests and prophets Jeremiah does not deserve a death sentence since he speaks in the name of the Lord, the God of the Israelites. The elders defend Jeremiah, recalling that Hezekiah, a king of Judah, did not condemn Jeremiah when he prophesied, "Zion shall be plowed as a field, Jerusalem a heap of ruins, and the Temple mount a forest ridge" (26:18). Hezekiah saves Jeremiah from death, fearing the Lord and seeking the Lord's favor. His hope was to persuade the Lord to forgive the nation.

In contrast to the story of Jeremiah being spared from death, the text contains the story of a prophet named Uriah who prophesied in the name of the Lord the same message of destruction as Jeremiah. King Jehoiakim sought to have Uriah killed for his message, but Uriah fled to Egypt. Some men captured Uriah and brought him back to Jehoiakim, who killed him with the sword and threw his corpse into a common burial ground.

In chapter 27, the Lord tells Jeremiah to deliver a message to the kings who are planning a rebellion against Babylon. The passage appears to refer to the period a few years before the Babylonian invasion in 587 BC when these nations, who were vassals of Babylon, planned to free themselves from the yoke of Babylon. Jeremiah urges the people to serve the king of Babylon until the time the king of Babylon shall be enslaved. The Lord will destroy with the sword, famine, and plague all those who do not accept the yoke of Babylon.

Jeremiah warns the people not to listen to their prophets and sorcerers who urge them not to serve the king of Babylon. The Lord promises to leave in peace the people who serve the king of Babylon. Jeremiah preaches the same message of warning to Zedekiah, warning him not to listen to the false prophets.

Jeremiah preaches the same message to the priests and all the people, telling them not to listen to their prophets who claim the vessels of the Temple will be brought back from Babylon. He notes if they were prophets and the Word of the Lord was with them, they would intercede with the Lord to protect the remaining vessels.

### Lectio Divina

Spend 8 to 10 minutes in silent contemplation of the following passage:

Jeremiah came close to being killed for spreading the Lord's message. Christians throughout the world who are working for the dignity and needs of the poor against unjust oppression face a similar threat. Some have already faced death in their quest to help the poor. Those who courageously speak out in the name of the Lord often find themselves unwelcome in an unjust society.

✠ *What can I learn from this passage?*

## Day 3: The Letter to the Exiles in Babylon (28—29)

A false prophet named Hananiah tells the priests and all the people in the Temple that within two years the Lord will break the yoke of the king of Babylon. At that time, Jeconiah, king of Judah, and all in exile will return along with the vessels Nebuchadnezzar took from Judah. Hananiah breaks the yoke from the neck of Jeremiah, saying the Lord will break the yoke of the king of Babylon from all nations within two years.

The Lord tells Jeremiah to inform Hananiah an iron yoke would be placed on the neck of the nations serving the king of Babylon, and even the wild beasts will serve the king. This is another way of saying nothing in the land escapes from the yoke of Babylon. Jeremiah confronted Hananiah, saying because he led the people astray, he will die that year. It happened as Jeremiah predicted.

Jeremiah sent a scroll to the remaining elders, priests, prophets, and people in exile in Babylon. Those in exile included King Jeconiah, the queen mother, the court officials, the princes of Judah and Jerusalem, and the artisans and smiths. In his scroll, Jeremiah speaks of the Lord's desire for the people to settle in Babylon as peacefully as possible. The Lord intends to keep alive a remnant of people who will return to Judah and Jerusalem when the Lord destroys the power of Babylon. They are to live normal lives, growing food and building homes and families while on exile. Surprisingly, the Lord tells them to work and pray for the welfare of the city of their exile.

The Lord predicts the Israelites will return to their homeland after seventy years in exile. When the people seek the Lord with their whole heart, the Lord will bring them home from all the nations and places to which the Lord banished them. The king and all the people in Jerusalem who did not go into exile will be killed by the sword, famine, or plague.

The Lord is handing over two false prophets, Ahab and Zedekiah, to the king of Babylon, who will roast them before the eyes of the people. Burning was a common, painful form of the death penalty used by the Babylonians. Shemaiah, a false prophet, sent a document to the people of Jerusalem, Zephaniah, and all the priests, urging Zephaniah to put Jeremiah in stocks for posing as a prophet. Zephaniah read the letter to Jeremiah, who then replied to the people in exile, telling them Shemaiah was a false prophet who led them astray.

### *Lectio Divina*

Spend 8 to 10 minutes in silent contemplation of the following passage:

> False prophets will always be with us. In the world today, many false prophets reinterpret the Words of the Lord in the Scripture to fit their manner of life or to offer false hope to those who are living a life contrary to the message of Christ. The message of such false prophets is easier to accept, but the story of Jeremiah warns the interpretations of such false prophets can have dire spiritual effects on people's life.

✠ *What can I learn from this passage?*

## Day 4: The Restoration (30—32)

Commentators view these chapters as containing a comforting message of return for the people of Judah and Jerusalem, and they titled this section "The Book of Comfort." Much of what appears in these passages comes from a later author who apparently wishes to lighten some of Jeremiah's predictions of doom with predictions of God's comforting guidance in bringing the exiles back to their homeland.

The first seven verses of chapter 30 appear to belong to the message of doom found in portions of Jeremiah's writings. The Lord hears the cry coming from the men in exile, which sounds like the cries of women in labor. Color drains from their face, signs of the great agony they are enduring.

Words of comfort come as the Lord declares the yoke of Babylon shall be broken and the bonds shall snap. Jacob (the Israelites) need not fear, for the Lord will soon deliver them. Although the Lord will punish Jacob as the nation deserves, the Lord will not destroy it. Instead, the Lord says, "I will bring to an end all the nations among whom I have scattered you" (30:11). The wound of the descendants is incurable, and the injury they caused by aligning themselves with foreign gods and powers is severe. Despite the suffering endured by the people of Judah, those who devour and plunder them will be devoured and plundered.

The Israelites were once called outcasts, but the Lord will rebuild a city (a possible reference to Jerusalem) on the old ruins. The Lord will increase the offspring of Jacob and glorify them, punishing all who oppress them. The leader of the people shall no longer be from a foreign nation but one of their own. The Lord will restore Judah and Jerusalem. The people will realize God is the true God of Israel and they are God's people. Those who escaped the sword shall find favor with the Lord as they come from far away to Jerusalem to receive rest. "A day will come" when the watchmen (prophets) call out on Mount Ephraim: "'Come, let us go up to Zion, to the Lord, our God'" (31:6). Everyone—the blind and the lame, pregnant women, laborers—will weep for joy as they travel to Jerusalem. The Lord shows compassion toward his people, leading them to streams of water, on a level road. All nations shall know the Lord; he who once scattered the people of Jacob will gather them together as a shepherd gathers his flock.

The people and the land shall blossom like a well-watered garden, with their young men and women dancing.

Jeremiah speaks of Rachel, the wife of Jacob and mother of Joseph and Benjamin, whose tomb many ancients believe was in Ramah. Ramah was the place where the Israelites were gathered before they were led into exile by the Babylonians. Rachel, from her tomb, weeps for her children who were being led into exile, and her grief is so intense she refuses to be consoled. The Lord tells her to cease weeping because her children shall return from exile to their own territory.

The name of Ephraim, one of the sons of Joseph, became synonymous with the nation of Israel. Ephraim repents and the Lord calls Ephraim a favored son. The Lord beckons all the people to return without hesitation. In the land of Judah, the farmers and sheepherders shall dwell together. Jeremiah presents a new covenant between God and the people after their return from exile, a covenant that will differ from the covenant the Lord made with Moses during the Exodus. Instead of being an external law, this new covenant will be founded on the law within the hearts of the people.

Jeremiah returns to the rebuilding of the city, establishing the boundaries of Jerusalem that are similar to those found in the Book of Nehemiah, which describes the people's rebuilding of the city. The Lord promises the city will never again be destroyed.

Chapter 32 begins with Jeremiah imprisoned by King Zedekiah of Judah because Jeremiah predicted the Lord was handing the city over to Babylon, and Zedekiah would be exiled to Babylon. A cousin of Jeremiah asserted Jeremiah, as his nearest relative, had the right to purchase land in Jeremiah's birthplace, Anathoth. Jeremiah purchased the land and gave the deed of purchase to Baruch in the presence of witnesses. Although the threat of destruction lay over the cities of Judah, Jeremiah purchased it to show the day of rebuilding would come. The Lord commanded him to put the deeds in an earthen jar where they would remain for a long time until the period of restoration began and the people again purchased houses, fields, and vineyards in the area.

## *Lectio Divina*

Spend 8 to 10 minutes in silent contemplation of the following passage:

> The author of the Gospel of Matthew was a Christian Jew who believed the events found in the Old Testament can be applied to events of his own era. In Jeremiah, we read Rachel wept for her children going into exile, while Matthew applies the quotation to Rachel weeping for the death of the innocents by Herod at the time Jesus was born (see Matthew 2:16–18). Jesus said, "Blessed are they who mourn" (Matthew 5:4). We can all mourn over the suffering and afflictions endured by others. Suffering is a universally shared experience.

✠ *What can I learn from this passage?*

---

## Day 5: The Restoration of Jerusalem (33—35)

The Word of the Lord came to Jeremiah while he was still under guard. The houses in the city and the house of the king of Judah were being torn down for the sake of defending the city against the Babylonians. As a result of the wrath of the Lord, many men will be killed defending the city. The Lord, however, promises to restore and heal the city, purifying the people of their guilt and forgiving them. The restoration will fill the Lord with joy and bring the Lord the praise of the nations witnessing this recovery.

The Lord speaks again to Jeremiah about the desolation of Jerusalem, but the Lord promises that songs of joy, gladness, weddings, and those bringing offerings to the Temple will again be heard. In another message to Jeremiah, the Lord speaks of the land as a waste, without people and animals, but states flocks and their shepherds shall again inhabit the land. The Lord promises, "I will make a just shoot rise up for David," a righteous leader (33:15). This appears to refer to all the kings of the line of David. The kingly line of David will not lack a successor, and the priests of Levi shall not lack descendants to sacrifice and make offerings on behalf of the people.

Jeremiah proclaims the Lord's promise is as stable as the Lord's covenants with day and night. The descendants of the Israelites will not be able to be counted, and they shall be as numerous as the heavenly bodies and the sands of the sea. The tribes of Benjamin and Judah shall survive.

Using the image again, he declares the Lord will save the tribes as surely as the Lord has established laws for the heavens and earth. The Lord will restore the kingship and priesthood forever.

In chapter 34, the Lord sends Jeremiah to King Zedekiah of Judah to tell him the Lord is turning the city over to the king of Babylon who will set it on fire, and Zedekiah himself has no means of escape but will see the Babylonian king face to face. The Lord promises Zedekiah he will not die by the sword but will die in peace and receive the ordinary burial reserved for kings. When Babylon was harassing the land of Judah but not yet seizing it, Zedekiah made a covenant with the people to have them free all their Hebrew slaves. The princes and people agreed to free their Judahite slaves, Jewish slaves who often indebted themselves to a master for food. When a lull in the siege took place, they broke the covenant made with Zedekiah and took their slaves back into slavery.

The Lord reminds Jeremiah of the covenant made when Israel's ancestors left Egypt to free all Hebrew slaves after six years of servitude. Just as their ancestors ignored the law, so the people of Jeremiah's day did the same after first allowing the slaves to go free and then taking them back into slavery. Since the people did not obey the Lord, the Lord will punish them with the sword, famine, and disease, making them a horror to all nations. The cities of Judah will become an uninhabited wasteland.

In chapter 35, the Lord directed Jeremiah to go to the house of the Rechabites. The Rechabites were a traditionalist group in Judah that refused to settle in the Promised Land like the other Hebrews and continued their nomadic form of life while remaining faithful to the covenant. Jeremiah is to bring them to one of the rooms in the Temple and give them wine. When Jeremiah fulfills this directive of the Lord and places wine in front of them, they inform him they do not drink wine. Their ancestor, Jonadab, the son of Rechab, commanded them not to drink wine, build houses, sow seeds, plant vineyards, or own them. They were to live in tents as aliens in the land. They state they had followed all these commands of Rechab's son. They moved into Jerusalem only when the Babylonians invaded the land.

The Lord then told Jeremiah to confront the people of Judah and the inhabitants of Jerusalem, asking why they refuse to accept correction and obey the Lord. The Lord points to the Rechabites as an example of faithful followers of their ancestors. As a result of the disobedience of the people of Judah and Jerusalem, the Lord will punish them as the Lord promised. Because the Rechabites obeyed the command of Jonadab, their father, the Lord, the God of Israel, assures them there will always be a descendant of Jonadab standing in the Lord's presence.

### *Lectio Divina*

Spend 8 to 10 minutes in silent contemplation of the following passage:

> The people in exile were helpless and weak, with no hope of returning to their Promised Land, but the Lord gave them hope, telling them a day would come when they would be free from the yoke of the Babylonians. Like the concentration camp survivors who hoped they would be freed, the people in exile in Babylon had hope some day they would be free—because the Lord promised them.

✠ *What can I learn from this passage?*

## Review Questions

1. What is the meaning of the imagery used by the Lord of the two baskets of figs?

2. Why does the author show a contrast between the life of Jeremiah and the life of the prophet Uriah?

3. What does Jeremiah mean when he tells the people to serve Babylon or perish?

# The Book of Jeremiah (III)

## JEREMIAH 36—52

*Thus says the LORD of hosts; The walls of spacious Babylon shall be leveled to the ground, its lofty gates destroyed by fire. The toil of the peoples is for nothing; the nations weary themselves for what the flames consume (51:58).*

**Opening Prayer** (SEE PAGE 16)

## Context

**Part 1: Jeremiah 36—38** Jeremiah dictates a scroll to Baruch, who reads it in the Temple area before the people. When the king of Judah receives the scroll, he has it burned because of its dire predictions against Jerusalem. Jeremiah dictates a second scroll to Baruch that contains all that was written in the first. In the meantime, Jeremiah endures prison in a dungeon and is thrown into a muddy cistern, but King Zedekiah orders his release.

**Part 2: Isaiah 39—52** Jerusalem is captured, and Nebuchadnezzar appoints Gedaliah as ruler of the cities of Judah. Jeremiah opts to remain in Judah under Gedaliah, but the ruler is eventually assassinated, and Jeremiah flees to Egypt. He continues to speak to the remnant remaining in Judah on behalf of the Lord, but the remnant refuses to believe Jeremiah's word. The remnant escapes to Egypt where they meet their death. The book ends with oracles against the nations and a short historical appendix that speaks of the capture and destruction of Jerusalem.

Read aloud Jeremiah 36—38.

### 36—37 Jeremiah's Scroll

Jeremiah calls upon Baruch to write a message concerning Judah and all the nations that the Lord ordered him to put in writing. Jeremiah tells us this happened in the fourth year of Jehoiakim, which would date the event as taking place around 605 BC. Baruch then brings the scroll to the Temple and reads it before the people. Apparently some event is taking place in the Temple, drawing crowds from surrounding areas to Jerusalem for prayer and fasting. For some unknown reason, Jeremiah is barred from entering the Temple.

Baruch reads the scroll from a window opening in a room overlooking the court of the Temple. During this period, certain favored families had the right to rooms in or near the Temple. Gemariah, a friend of Jeremiah, had a right to the room overlooking the court of the Temple. A son of Gemariah, named Micaiah, hears the reading of the scroll and reports all he heard to princes at a meeting in the house of the king who was not present at the time. The alarmed princes meet with Baruch and instruct him to read the scroll in their presence. When Baruch finishes reading and tells the princes these were the words Jeremiah dictated to him, the princes decide they have to tell the king. Meanwhile, they advise Baruch and Jeremiah to go into hiding.

The princes report about the scroll to the king, who is sitting in his winter house with a fire burning in a brazier in front of him. The king orders a servant to bring the scroll and to read it to him. As the servant finishes reading three or four columns, he (the servant) would cut off the piece with his scribe's knife, which was ordinarily used to sharpen reeds for writing, and throw the pieces of the scroll into the fire. Despite the objections of three of the princes, the king continues to have the scroll consumed in the fire. When the servant finishes reading the scroll, the king orders the arrest of Baruch and Jeremiah, but the Lord hid them.

After the king burns the scroll, the Lord directs Jeremiah to dictate to Baruch all the words of the first scroll and to tell the king, as a result of burning the scroll, no descendant of his shall occupy the throne of David. The Lord predicts Jehoiakim's corpse would be thrown out, totally exposed to heat by day and frost by night. Jeremiah gives Baruch a new scroll and dictates the same words contained in the first scroll.

Nebuchadnezzar, the king of Babylon, appoints Zedekiah king over the land of Judah. Zedekiah sends a messenger to Jeremiah, requesting him to plead with the Lord for the nation. Meanwhile, the Babylonians retreat from Jerusalem when word reaches them that Pharaoh's army is leaving Egypt to join in the defense of the city. The Lord instructs Jeremiah to inform King Zedekiah's messengers that Pharaoh's army, which set out to help them, will return to Egypt, and the Babylonians will then return and annihilate Jerusalem by setting the city on fire.

Jeremiah leaves Jerusalem to visit the territory of Benjamin to receive his share of property from among the people. The captain of the guard at the Gate of Benjamin, however, arrests Jeremiah, accusing him of deserting to the Babylonians. Although Jeremiah keeps denying the accusation, the captain of the guard brings him to the princes who, have him beaten and imprisoned in the home of Jonathan, a scribe, whose house is being used as a prison. Jeremiah remains in a dungeon in the house for a number of days.

King Zedekiah orders his servants to bring Jeremiah to his palace. The king secretly asks Jeremiah if he had any word from the Lord. Jeremiah responds that King Zedekiah will be handed over to the king of Babylon. After he finishes warning Zedekiah, he pleads with the king not to send him back to the dungeon, where he would surely die, so Zedekiah sends him to the court of the guard, where he receives a ration of bread each day until all the bread in the city is consumed.

### 38:1–28 Jeremiah in the Muddy Cistern

Jeremiah preaches that those who remain in the city of Jerusalem shall die by the sword, famine, or plague, while those who go out to Babylon shall live. Because the princes believe Jeremiah was weakening the resolve of the soldiers and the people remaining in the city, they want him killed. As a result, they lower Jeremiah into a muddy cistern with no water. Jeremiah sinks into the mud.

An Ethiopian, a court official in the king's house, pleads with the king to have Jeremiah lifted from the cistern, saying Jeremiah would die of starvation since there is no more bread in the city. The king instructs the Ethiopian to get three men and lift Jeremiah out of the cistern. Jeremiah, however, remains in custody in the court of the guard.

Zedekiah summons Jeremiah to question him concerning the Word of the Lord. When he tells Jeremiah not to hide anything from him, Jeremiah asks if the king will spare him if he tells what the Lord has said. The king swears not to kill him or hand him over to the men who wish to kill him. Jeremiah tells the king if he surrenders to the princes of Babylon's king, he and his household will not die and the city will not be destroyed by fire. If the king does not surrender to the Babylonians, then the Babylonians will set fire to the city and Zedekiah will not escape from them.

Zedekiah fears the consequences of surrender, believing the Babylonians would turn him over to the Judahites, a group of Jews who joined the Babylonians. Jeremiah promises the king will not be handed over to them. When the king refuses to listen to Jeremiah, Jeremiah relates a vision of women in the house of the king being brought out to the princes of Babylon, crying out as they went, saying Jeremiah's good friends betrayed him, allowing his feet to sink in the mud.

Zedekiah warns Jeremiah not to tell anyone about their conversation. If the princes were to ask what Jeremiah and the king spoke about, Jeremiah is to answer he pleaded with the king not to send him back to Jonathan's house lest he die there. Jeremiah remains in the court of the guard until the day the Babylonians capture Jerusalem.

## Review Questions

1. Who was Baruch?
2. Why did the king allow the scroll of Jeremiah to be burned?
3. Why did the people want to kill Jeremiah?

---

**Closing Prayer** (SEE PAGE 16)

Pray the closing prayer now or after *lectio divina*.

### *Lectio Divina* (SEE PAGE 9)

Relax your body and maintain a posture of prayer (back straight, eyes shut, feet flat on the floor). This exercise can take as long as you want, but in the context of this Bible study, 10 to 20 minutes should be sufficient.

The meditations that follow are provided only to help group participants use this prayer form, but note that *lectio* is intended to bring one to a place of prayerful contemplation where the Word of God speaks to the hearer from his or her heart. (See page 9 for further instruction.)

### *Jeremiah's Scroll (36—37)*

Jeremiah, who preached the warnings of the Lord, became an unwelcome prophet in Judah. When Jesus predicted the destruction of the Temple just as Jeremiah did, Jesus, who is God, became an unwelcome prophet in Jerusalem. Archbishop Oscar Romero became an unwelcome prophet in San Salvador when he ordered the soldiers to stop killing innocent people. Each one of these prophets courageously endured suffering and death for sharing the Word of the Lord. They are models of bravery and dedication for all believers.

✠ *What can I learn from this passage?*

### *Jeremiah in the Muddy Cistern (38:1–28)*

Although Jeremiah predicted bad news for the city of Jerusalem and for Judah, he also predicted good news, which the leaders of the people refused to hear. He told them the captives taken to Babylon would live and eventually a remnant would return to rebuild Jerusalem and Judah. Jesus preached about his suffering and death, but he always added the good news that he would be raised on the third day. He also promised we, too, would share in a resurrection. Like Jesus, we may have to be willing to suffer and even die in remaining faithful to the Lord, but we remain faithful because we are aware of the good news of resurrection.

✠ *What can I learn from this passage?*

# PART 2: INDIVIDUAL STUDY (39—52)

## Day 1: The Capture of Jerusalem (39—41)

When the king of Babylon and his army lay siege to the city of Jerusalem, Zedekiah and his warriors attempt to flee the city at night, but the Babylonians (Chaldeans) capture them. They bring Zedekiah to the king of Babylon, who executes Zedekiah's sons before his eyes and all the king's nobles. As predicted, he blinds Zedekiah and brings him in chains to Babylon.

The Babylonians burn the homes of the people and tear down the walls of Jerusalem. The captain of the bodyguard deports to Babylon the people remaining in Jerusalem, including those who deserted to him and the rest of the workers, leaving behind some of the poor to whom he gives the vineyards and farms.

The king of Babylon gives orders that nothing is to happen to Jeremiah. They take him out of the courtyard of the guard and put him in Gedaliah's trust, leaving him in Jerusalem. Before his release from the courtyard of the guard, Jeremiah tells the Ethiopian, who previously pleaded with the king to free Jeremiah from the muddy cistern, that he (the Ethiopian) would not be handed over to the Babylonians, and he will escape.

In chapter 40, the captain of the bodyguard gives Jeremiah an option to come with him to Babylon or remain in Jerusalem. He informs Jeremiah he could go wherever he wished, or he could go to Gedaliah whom the king of Babylon set over the cities of Judah. Jeremiah chooses to go to Gedaliah and dwell with him among the people left behind in Jerusalem. Because Jerusalem was in such a shambles, Gedaliah chooses to live in Mizpah, a city in Judah near Jerusalem.

When the military leaders remaining with their soldiers hear the king of Babylon set Gedaliah over them and the people remaining in Jerusalem, they come to Gedaliah, who swears that all will go well with them if they serve the king of Babylon. Gedaliah instructs the people to harvest the wine, the fruit, and the oil and to store them in jars. When the Judahites in Moab, Ammon, Edom, and those scattered in other foreign lands learn that the king of Babylon left a remnant in Judah with Gedaliah as their leader, they return to Judah and enjoy a rich harvest of wine and fruit.

A man named Johanan and other military leaders warn Gedaliah the Ammonite king sent a man named Ishmael to assassinate him. Johanan begs Gedaliah to allow him to go and secretly kill Ishmael, adding the death of Gedaliah would force the Judahites to flee and the remnant of Judah would perish. Gedaliah refuses to believe Johanan, telling him he was lying.

In chapter 41, Ishmael and ten of his men come to Gedaliah. While dining together, Ishmael and the ten men kill Gedaliah, the Judahites of military age who joined with Gedaliah, and the Babylonian soldiers stationed there. A day later, eighty men with beards shaved off, ragged clothing, and gashes in their bodies as signs of repentance for their sins against the Lord arrive from Shiloh and Samaria. They bring incense and grain offerings for the Temple. At the time, no one yet knew about the death of Gedaliah. Ishmael meets them weeping, but once the men are inside the city, Ishmael and his soldiers slaughter them, filling a large cistern with their corpses.

When Johanan and the army leaders with him hear about the crimes Ishmael committed, they pursue him and his men. The captives with Ishmael rejoice and join with Johanan's forces. Ishmael manages to flee to the Ammonites with eight of his men. Because Johanan fears the anger of Babylonians over the assassination of Gedaliah, he flees with them and his army into Egypt.

### Lectio Divina

Spend 8 to 10 minutes in silent contemplation of the following passage:

A prophet is one who speaks in the name of the Lord. Jeremiah not only suffers because of the messages he delivers, but because he is caught in the middle between the Lord and the people. Jesus once said, "No prophet is accepted in his own native place" (Luke 4:24). In many areas, the message of the Lord is rejected, and the messenger may be challenged or killed.

✠ *What can I learn from this passage?*

## Day 2: The Conflict Spreads to Egypt (42—45)

Johanan and the remaining military leaders ask Jeremiah to speak to the Lord for them, hoping the Lord would guide them. When Jeremiah agrees, the leaders swear to follow all the instructions the Lord sent them through Jeremiah, whether or not they agree with the instructions. After a few days, Jeremiah tells them and all the people that the Lord will relent of the evil cast upon them and plant them in the land of Judah if they remain. If they disobey the Lord and go to Egypt expecting freedom from war and hunger, they will encounter the sword, hunger, plague, and death once they arrive there. Just as the Lord's wrath ravaged Jerusalem, so the fury of the Lord will inflict the remnant, making them a curse, an object of evil, horror, and disgrace.

In chapter 43, Johanan, the rest of the leaders, and the remnant of the people go to Egypt. They accuse Jeremiah of lying to them. The Lord directs Jeremiah to set some stones in mortar in the terrace at the entrance to the house of Pharaoh while the Judahites watch him. He is to tell the people the king of Babylon will establish his throne on these stones and stretch out a canopy over them, a sign the king of Babylon will rule Egypt. He (the king of Babylon) will ravage the land, burn the temples, cart the idols away, and pick Egypt clean just as a shepherd picks lice from his cloak. He shall depart victorious. This devastation of the land of Egypt took place around the year 568 BC.

The Lord questions why the Judahites inflicted evil on themselves by leading the people out of Judah without leaving even a remnant behind. They provoke the Lord further by worshiping the gods in the land of Egypt where they settled. The Lord asks if they wish to become a curse and disgrace in the eyes of other nations, questioning whether they forgot the evil actions of the people of Judah, who still refuse to show any fear of the Lord. The Lord informs the remnant in Egypt they, too, because of their disobedience, will be killed by the sword or die of hunger.

The women among the remnant refuse to listen to Jeremiah, claiming they had plenty to eat and did not suffer disaster when they made their offerings to Astarte, the queen of heaven, just as their ancestors did in Judah and Jerusalem. According to the people, disaster struck when they stopped offering sacrifices and oblations. Jeremiah refuses to accept this response. Just as the people did not listen to the Lord or obey his commands and experienced evil from the Lord, so the remnant will experience the same. With the exception of very few who will escape death in Egypt, the Lord will completely destroy them.

The Lord's punishment of the people will stand as a sign of the power of the Lord. The Lord promises to turn Pharaoh over to his enemies who are seeking his life, just as the Lord turned Zedekiah over to the king of Babylon who was seeking his life. When the scribe Baruch first hears the prophecy of the Lord concerning the destruction of Judah, he fears for his own life. The Lord, however, promises Baruch his life shall be spared.

### *Lectio Divina*

Spend 8 to 10 minutes in silent contemplation of the following passage:

At times, people make promises to the Lord when they become overwhelmed with sickness, family pressures, financial disasters, or some similar calamity. They promise to pray more or make specific sacrifices. When the calamity passes, however, many forget about their promises and live life as they did before the catastrophe began. We can learn from the people of Jeremiah's day that we should not make promises lightly, as Johanan did.

✠ *What can I learn from this passage?*

---

## Day 3: Oracles Against the Nations (46—48)

Although the Book of Jeremiah introduces a series of oracles against foreign nations in chapters 46 through 51, the events in the series are not in chronological order.

Jeremiah begins his proclamation with an oracle of the Lord against Egypt. In 605 BC, the king of Babylon thwarted the Egyptian plans for conquering other nations when he defeated the Egyptian army near the Euphrates River. The Egyptian army was prepared for war, moving forward with shields ready, horses harnessed, helmets in place, spears set, and well-armored warriors. Despite the preparation, they panic in terror before the Babylonians, fleeing without making a stand. Even the fastest cannot escape, stumbling and falling on the banks of the river. Egypt boasted it had plans to inundate the land like the surging waters of the Nile, but in the north the Lord seeks vengeance. The swords of the Babylonians are drunk with the blood of the enemy. Virgin Egypt will find no balm, no healing. It was a custom in ancient times to refer to a nation as a woman.

The king of Babylon reached Egypt, possibly in 604 BC. Jeremiah speaks of the bull-god named Apis fleeing because the Lord thrust him down. The people of ancient times often saw battles between nations as a battle between their gods. The image of the bull-god in flight witnesses to the power of the Lord. The Babylonians return home, possibly to protect their homeland. Pharaoh receives the name of humiliation, "Braggart-missed-his-chance," which is a reference to the fallen pride of Pharaoh.

The Lord comes above the highest mountains, calling the Egyptians to prepare for exile, leaving southern Egypt as a wasteland behind them. Egypt, like a beautiful heifer, must contend with the horseflies from the north, a reference to the aggravating attacks from the north. Everyone flees as the enemy, the Babylonians, come with fury like a countless swarm of men who carry axes to cut down the trees of a forest, no matter how impenetrable. In shame, daughter Egypt is handed over to the people from the north.

The Lord of hosts proclaims punishment for Amon of Thebes, a god of northern Egypt, and all the gods, kings, Pharaoh, and those who trust him. The Lord will hand them over to Nebuchadnezzar, king of Babylon, and to his officers.

The oracle of the Lord shifts to Jacob, urging the people not to fear because the Lord promises to deliver their offspring from the lands of their exile. The Lord will bring an end to the nations to which the family of Jacob was banished, but Jacob shall survive.

In chapter 47, Jeremiah proclaims an oracle against the Philistines, which appears to be a reference to Nebuchadnezzar's attack against the Philistines in 604 BC. The Lord speaks of waters from the north flooding the land, the cities, and the inhabitants. The passage speaks of images of the pounding hooves of horses, the clanking chariots, the rumbling wheels, all meant to point to the onslaught of the Babylonians. The terror is so great, parents do not turn back for their children. The Philistines are isolated from their allies, the Phoenician cities of Tyre and Sidon. Baldness, used as an image of lamentation by the ancients, covers the people as city after city is conquered. The people cry out for the Lord to put away his sword, but they doubt this bloodshed can end since the Lord has commanded it.

Chapter 48 contains an oracle of the Lord against Moab, a territory east of the Dead Sea. The oracle begins by including the end of smaller towns of Moab. With their destruction came the end the glory of Moab as a nation. The text speaks of silencing "Madmen," which is apparently the name of a town. The people must flee to save their lives. Chemosh, the god of Moab, shall go into exile with his priests and princes. Moab will become a wasteland, like a graveyard.

From the beginning, Moab has been complacent, resting from the time of its youth, never having to endure exile. The wine of Moab was famous for its flavor, but it is now the source of the city's downfall. The Lord will send winemakers to decant the wine, empty its flasks, and shatter its jars. The god Chemosh shall disillusion Moab, just as the god Bethel (not the city) disillusioned the Israelites who worshiped the false god.

The Lord asks how the people of Moab can brag they are powerful warriors. The one who ravages Moab and its cities, namely Babylon, slaughters the best of their youth. The Lord curses Moab, predicting it will swim in its own vomit and become a laughingstock. The Lord urges the people of Moab to flee from the cities and hide in the crags like a dove nesting in the walls of a gorge. The destruction of the cities of Moab and their people is a reason for wailing and crying.

The Lord declares no one will be left in Moab to offer burnt offerings or to sacrifice to their gods. The people mourn with every head shaved bald, every beard cut off, every hand gashed, and wearing sackcloth. The Babylonians will sweep down on Moab like an eagle spreading its wings, capturing cities and strongholds. Because Moab set itself against the Lord, the Lord will wipe it out. Although the Moabites will be taken into exile, the Lord promises to restore the fortunes of Moab in the future.

## *Lectio Divina*

Spend 8 to 10 minutes in silent contemplation of the following passage:

> The Lord hates the arrogant who forget their power comes from the Lord. Egypt and Moab were strong nations boasting of their power. The Lord will humiliate them. People who boast of their powers soon learn most people find them difficult to befriend. Our gifts come from the Lord, and we must trust the Lord to continue to guide us in the use of our gifts.

✠ *What can I learn from this passage?*

---

## Day 4: The Word of the Lord Against the Nations (49—50)

After the Assyrians destroyed the northern kingdom of Israel, no Israelite was left to claim the land, so the Ammonites occupied the territory. Jeremiah proclaims the Lord's oracle against the Ammonites. The national god of the Ammonites was Milcom, who supplanted the worship of the Lord of Israel in the territory of the northern kingdom. As a result, the Lord will sound the battle alarm against Rabbah, the capital of Ammon, and destroy it. Milcom will go into exile with the priests and princes of the land. The Lord, however, will restore their fortunes in time.

Jeremiah proclaims the Lord's oracle against Edom, also known as Esau, the brother of Jacob (see Genesis 36:1). The nation of Edom took advantage of the Babylonian invasion of Judah and captured a southern portion of Judah that was too weak to defend itself. The Lord asks if there is any wisdom in Teman, a district of Edom that is representative of the whole country. Bozrah, the capital of Edom, and all cities of Edom will be destroyed, making them places of horror, disgrace, desolation, and a curse.

The insertion of an oracle against Damascus is confusing, since it occurred before Jeremiah's era, in the late eighth century before Christ, although the armies of Damascus caused consternation for the Israelites. The enemy of Damascus is coming from the north. The people of Damascus panic and wail like a woman in labor over the impending doom of the once powerful and invincible Damascus. Now its young men and warriors will fall on the same day, and fire shall destroy the palaces of the kings.

The Lord declares an oracle against Kedar and Hazor, areas in Arabia. The people of Kedar were a semi-nomadic group who lived mostly in tents. The oracle speaks of destroying the people from the east, their tents, and their flocks. They flee on their camels to avoid the terror. Nebuchadnezzar easily ravaged the city, which was unguarded.

Jeremiah proclaims an oracle of the Lord against Elam at the beginning of the reign of Zedekiah, which would place the oracle around 587 BC. The message of the Lord declares the destruction of the bow of Elam. The Elamites were noted for their prowess with the bow and arrow. Like other nations before them, Elam will be terrified at the onslaught of the Babylonians. The Lord promises to restore the fortunes of Elam as the Lord promised other nations.

Chapters 50 and 51 contain a collection of oracles against Babylon. Some of the oracles speak of the fall of Babylon being completed, while others speak of the fall of Babylon as a future event. The oracles begin with the Lord's call to the nations, announcing the news about the fall of Bel, a god in Babylon, and Marduk, the great god of Babylon. Viewing the war between nations as a war between the gods of those nations, Jeremiah links the fall of Babylon with the fall of the gods of Babylon.

Jeremiah speaks of a nation from the north advancing against Babylon. This may or may not be a reference to Cyrus, the king of Persia, who eventually conquered Babylon. The enemy from the north shall ravage Babylon and leave it desolate.

Then Jeremiah shifts his attention to the Judahites and Israelites, saying they shall join together, weeping as they return to the Lord and committing themselves to an eternal covenant with the Lord. The Lord speaks of the people of Judah and Israel as lost sheep, led astray by their shepherds. Their enemies reject any accusations of guilt, saying the punishment of the people came as a result of their sins against the Lord. Because the nations of the north are advancing, the Lord urges the Israelites to flee from Babylon as quickly as possible. The nations will conquer and plunder Babylon.

The oracle refers to Babylon as a mother, saying the mother of the Chaldeans shall be put to shame and the land left desolate as a result of the Lord's wrath. The Lord directs the nations to surround Babylon, shower it with arrows, and shout out the war cry. The nations destroy all the fortifications and walls of the city, causing the Chaldeans to surrender. The Lord, however, seeks retribution, telling the nations to treat Babylon in the same manner Babylon treated other nations.

Jeremiah again shifts his message to the Israelites, saying they were like sheep pursued by lions. They were first demolished by the king of Assyria and recently by the king of Babylon. The Lord promises to punish the king of Babylon as the Lord punished the king of Assyria and bring the Israelites back to their fertile land. He notes Israel's and Judah's oppression. The mighty Lord defends their cause and allows the land of Israel and Judah a period of rest.

The oracle returns against Babylon, telling those attacking Babylon to slaughter all the people in the cities, putting them under the ban. The wrath of the Lord unleashes every weapon against them, not even allowing a remnant to survive. The Lord has broken the once-mighty hammer of Babylon. They insulted the Lord when they destroyed the Temple in Jerusalem, and now they will be punished for their insolence against the Lord's people.

The Lord will destroy the Chaldeans. The sword shall devour all, and a drought shall dry up the waters of the land, a land of idols soon to be a land of phantoms. The Lord will treat Babylon in the same manner the Lord treated Sodom and Gomorrah and their neighbors, leaving a wasteland in its place.

Verses 44—46 of chapter 50 are similar to those in 49:19–22 with the exception of the change of the name of the area being devastated. The Lord will come up like a lion "from the Jordan's thicket" to establish all the Lord chooses. Who can hold the Lord accountable? "What shepherd [leader] can stand against me?" the Lord asks. In his plan, the people and flocks of Babylon shall be dragged away. The news Babylon is captured will be as shocking as an earthquake.

### Lectio Divina

Spend 8 to 10 minutes in silent contemplation of the following passage:

The Lord works in revealed, concealed ways. When we pray for a warm day and receive it, we may wonder if it would have happened the same way if we had not prayed. When the Israelites prayed for the Lord to deliver them from the Babylonians, many among them may have wondered if the defeat of the Babylonians would have taken place, even if they did not pray. People of faith believe the Lord responds to prayer, and most of the time the answer comes in a revealed, concealed way.

✠ *What can I learn from this passage?*

## Day 5: The Second Oracle Against Babylon (51—52)

In chapter 51, Jeremiah passes on another oracle of the Lord against Babylon, similar in many ways to that found in chapter 50. The Lord will stir up against Babylon a destroyer wind, which is a reference to a severe, dry wind from the east. Like grain that is winnowed, Babylon will be cut down. The enemy will surround Babylon with the intention of putting everyone under the ban, meaning everyone, young and old, must be killed.

The Lord of hosts will remain with the Israelites. Since the Lord is about to destroy Babylon for its guilt, the Lord urges the people of Israel and Judah to flee from Babylon to save their lives. The Lord placed a golden cup of vengeance in the hands of the Babylonians, and they made the nations drink of its destructive wine. The Lord tried to heal the wounds of Babylon, but Babylon could not be healed.

The Lord has roused up the king of the Medes for the destruction of Babylon. Later in history (549 BC), the Persians will make the land of the Medes one of its provinces. The reference to the king of the Medes could be a reference to the king of Persia who destroyed Babylon. The destruction of Babylon is the Lord's retribution for all the evil it committed.

The Lord rebukes the stupidity of those who make lifeless idols. The Lord is mighty, an editor adds, for he created the earth, the world, the heavens, thunder, clouds, lightning, rain, and wind. The people of Israel and Judah, unlike the Babylonians, worship the Lord, "the creator of all things" (51:19).

Jeremiah pictures Jerusalem as lamenting over the destruction caused by the king of Babylon that left the city like an empty vessel. Zion seeks revenge, calling upon the Lord to allow the wounds suffered by the nation to be visited upon the Babylonians. The Lord promises to avenge Jerusalem, making Babylon a mound of ruins, totally desolated. When they cry out for drink, the Lord will make them drunk with eternal sleep. The Lord will lead the Babylonians like lambs, rams, and goats to the slaughter.

The Lord urges the people of Zion to remember Jerusalem and return home. Babylon is destroyed because of its disgraceful treatment of Jerusalem and the Temple. Even if Babylon uses her high places as fortifications, the Lord's army will still reach her. Their governors, officers, and warriors will sleep forever. The toil of the people in building the walls and gates to protect Babylon will come to nothing when these are leveled to the ground.

Jeremiah sends Seraiah, the brother of Baruch, to Babylon. The author speaks about a trip made by Zedekiah, the king of Judah, to Babylon, but the trip is not mentioned elsewhere. Perhaps Zedekiah went to Babylon to appease the king after the king heard about Zedekiah's intended rebellion against Babylon. Jeremiah wrote on a scroll about the disaster that would take place against the Babylonians. Jeremiah directed Seraiah to tie a stone around the scroll after he finished reading it aloud and throw it into the Euphrates River. Babylon will sink in the same manner, never to rise again.

In chapter 52, a later editor took a large portion of this chapter from 2 Kings 24:18—25:30. "Zedekiah was twenty-one years old when he became king; he reigned eleven years in Jerusalem....He did what was evil in the sight of the Lord, just as Jehoiakim had done" (52:1–2). Zedekiah foolishly rebelled against the king of Babylon, which led the king to lay siege to the city and capture it in the eleventh year of the reign of Zedekiah. Zedekiah and the soldiers attempted to escape the city in the midst of a famine but were captured. The king of Babylon slaughtered Zedekiah's sons before his eyes and then plucked out Zedekiah's eyes, bound him, and brought him to Babylon, where he remained until he died.

A short time later, the king of Babylon sent his captain of the bodyguard and a number of warriors to demolish Jerusalem, burning the house of the Lord, the house of the king, and all the houses of Jerusalem. The troops tore down the walls surrounding Jerusalem. The captain of the bodyguard led into exile the remnant of the people who were left, those who deserted the king of Babylon and the skilled workers. He left behind some of the poor as vinedressers and farmers.

The author describes in detail all the bronze, gold, and silver the Chaldeans took from the Temple. The captain of the guard also took Seraiah, the high priest, who was apparently not the brother of Baruch mentioned earlier in the Book of Jeremiah. He also took a number of leading people of Jerusalem to the king of Babylon, who executed them. Nebuchadnezzar exiled 3,023 people from Judah and 832 people from Jerusalem. The captain of the guard deported 745 Judahites. The number of exiles totaled 4,000 people.

The king who succeeded Nebuchadnezzar released Jehoiakim, king of Judah, from prison, spoke favorably of him, and raised him higher than all the other kings who were with him in Babylon. He ate at the king's table as long as he lived and received a perpetual, fixed daily allowance for the remainder of his life.

### Lectio Divina

Spend 8 to 10 minutes in silent contemplation of the following passage:

The Lord not only saves the Israelites but also punishes the nations causing devastation for Judah and Jerusalem. Jesus tells us not to seek revenge on those who hurt us but to leave vengeance to the Lord, to whom it belongs (see Deuteronomy 32:35). This demands trust in the Lord.

✠ *What can we learn from this passage?*

## Review Questions

1. Who was left in the city of Jerusalem after the Babylonian invasion? Why?
2. Why was the Lord displeased when the remnant left in Jerusalem fled to Egypt?
3. What was the mission Jeremiah gave to Seraiah?

# The Books of Lamentations and Baruch

## LAMENTATIONS 1—5 AND BARUCH 1—6

*How solitary sits the city, once filled with people. She who was great among the nations is now like a widow. Once a princess among the provinces, now a toiling slave (Lamentations 1:1).*

**Opening Prayer** (SEE PAGE 16)

## Context

**Part 1: Lamentations 1—2** The Book of Lamentations contains five poems lamenting the destruction of Jerusalem by the Babylonians in 587 BC. Although the poems were once believed to have been written by Jeremiah, this seems unlikely. The first two laments concern the desolation faced by Jerusalem and the Lord's wrath against that city.

**Part 2: Lamentations 3—5; Baruch 1—6** The poems in Lamentations express the grief of one living under the punishments of the Lord. The third lament is the voice of an individual who has known affliction. The author of the fourth lament mourns over the miseries endured by the people in Jerusalem, and the fifth lament grieves over the present situation of the people and begs the Lord to accept them back as in days past.

The Book of Baruch receives its identity from the opening lines that speak of Baruch reading the scroll in the presence of Jeconiah, son of Jehoiakim, king of Judah. The book contains four different compositions, a section on the wonders of wisdom, and ends with a letter attributed to Jeremiah. It recognizes the guilt of the people and the justice of God, and pleads for the Lord to show mercy to the people.

## PART 1: GROUP STUDY (LAMENTATIONS 1—2)

Read aloud Lamentations 1—2.

### 1:1–22 The Desolation of Jerusalem

The author of Lamentations speaks forlornly of the desolate city of Jerusalem that was once great among the nations and filled with people. Jerusalem is now like a widow or a lowly slave who weeps incessantly with no one to comfort her from among her lovers. Her lovers were the nations that once supported and protected Jerusalem. Judah has gone into exile, dwelling among the nations, oppressed and working under harsh conditions. The roads to Zion and the gates of the city that were once filled with travelers are empty. There are no more priests in the city.

Judah's glory has faded, and her once-glorious princes roam like rams in search of pastures. Because of her sins, those who once honored her now humiliate her. The enemy saw her nakedness, a reference to the punishment faced by accused prostitutes who were stripped naked. In turning to other gods, Jerusalem had become a prostitute in the Lord's eyes.

Jerusalem recognizes she has no future and witnesses the loss of her precious gifts, including those in the Temple. The people in exile sell all they have for bread and cry out to the Lord to witness their depravity. The Lord's wrath burned into their very bones, entrapped them, and left them desolate. The yoke of their rebellion against the Lord delivered them into the grasp of the enemy.

Jerusalem, like something unclean, weeps with no one to comfort her. Since Jerusalem defied the command of the Lord, the people must admit the Lord is justified. When the young women and men went into captivity, none of Jerusalem's lovers protected them, and all nations abandoned her.

Even the priests and elders scoured for food. Jerusalem groans, but her enemies rejoice over the affliction cast on them by the Lord. The people pray that the Lord will witness the enemy's evil and deal with them as brutally as the Lord dealt with Jerusalem.

### 2:1–22 The Lord's Wrath and Zion's Ruin

Because of Israel's sinfulness, the Lord no longer pays attention to the "footstool" of the Lord, a reference to the Ark of the Covenant, whose exterior design consisted of two angels on each side of a footstool (2:1). Since the people could not make an image of the Lord, they designed a footstool as the place where the Lord dwelt. In saying the Lord no longer remembers the footstool, the poet is saying the Lord has abandoned the Temple that housed the Ark of the Covenant.

The Lord acts without pity, demolishing Judah and Israel and no longer protecting the offspring of Jacob with all their kings and princes. Like an enemy warrior, the Lord bends the bow against the people of Judah and Israel, killing them and all they valued. The Lord destroys their defenses, causing lamentation throughout the land. The Lord rejects the Temple (the booth), the altar, and the sanctuary, and along with them, the ability of the people to celebrate feasts and Sabbaths. A boisterous shout like that heard on feast days fills the Temple as the conquering army celebrates and the people loudly lament.

The Lord extends the "measuring line," which was used for building or destroying (2:8). In this case, the measuring line plans the extent of the destruction. The gates of the city are smashed and fall to the ground. The Lord plans to destroy kings, princes, prophets, elders in mourning, and the young women bowing their heads toward the ground. The poet weeps and experiences anguish deep within his stomach. In the devastation, children and infants cry out to their mothers for bread and wine, and they die in their mothers' arms.

The devastation resulting from the sins of Judah and Israel is so overwhelming the Lord cannot adequately compare it to anything else. The prophets identified their guilt. All those who witness the destruction of Judah and Israel will hiss and wag their heads, asking where the glory of Jerusalem has gone, and rejoicing in the destruction of that once mighty city.

The horrors of the siege lead the people of Zion to wail day and night without rest. The people pray to the Lord to look upon the ruthlessness of the siege that leads women to eat their own offspring and the death of priests and prophets in the sanctuary of the Lord. The bodies of the people fill the streets, slaughtered without pity. No one survives.

## Review Questions

1. How does the past glory of Judah cause such pain in the present?
2. What does the author mean when he says the Lord has become like an enemy?
3. What does the author mean when he says the prophets have provided visions of whitewashed illusions?

---

**Closing Prayer** (SEE PAGE 16)

Pray the closing prayer now or after *lectio divina*.

---

**Lectio Divina** (SEE PAGE 9)

Relax your body and maintain a posture of prayer (back straight, eyes shut, feet flat on the floor). This exercise can take as long as you want, but in the context of this Bible study, 10 to 20 minutes should be sufficient.

The meditations that follow are provided only to help group participants use this prayer form, but note that *lectio* is intended to bring one to a place of prayerful contemplation where the Word of God speaks to the hearer from his or her heart. (See page 9 for further instruction.)

### The Desolation of Jerusalem (1:1–22)

The first lamentation recognizes the people of Judah have caused their own punishment by their sins, and the author lists all the reasons for lamenting with the hope the Lord will punish other nations as the Lord punished Judah. Many of the reasons for lamenting in our lives come as a result of our own weaknesses or faults. We should not be quick to blame others for our woes.

✠ *What can I learn from this passage?*

### The Lord's Wrath and Zion's Ruin (2:1–22)

The one lamenting realizes it is the sins of the people that have brought this devastation on themselves, but they never cease calling on the Lord to wake up and help them. When all seems hopeless, the one lamenting calls out to the Lord to pay attention to their plight. It is a prayer of hope.

✠ *What can I learn from this passage?*

## PART 2: INDIVIDUAL STUDY (LAMENTATIONS 3—5; BARUCH 1—6)

### Day 1: The Community Laments (Lamentations 3—5)

An unknown speaker laments his suffering. The lamentation refers to an individual who represents the suffering of the people and who still calls upon the Lord for help. The Lord has abandoned him, forcing him to walk in darkness. His flesh is decaying, his bones are broken, he endures poverty and hardship, and he lives in the darkness of death. The Lord has hemmed him in as though surrounding him with a wall of stones. He is like a man at the mercy of a bear or lion, being torn apart, and a target for arrows. The speaker is taunted and filled with bitterness, forced to eat gravel in a hopeless life, deprived of peace and happiness.

The tone changes to one of trusting the Lord. Despite the suffering, the man's hope still endures, trusting in the compassion of the Lord and the goodness of the Lord toward those who trust in the Lord God. The speaker hopes in silence for the Lord's deliverance, even when the weight upon him is heavy, forcing him to eat the dust and suffer the humiliation of turning his cheek to the enemy. Although the Lord brings grief, the Lord is still merciful, not happily casting grief on the people.

Whatever happens in the world takes place because the Lord allows it, whether the thing be "both good and bad" (3:38). The speaker beckons the people to examine themselves and admit they have rebelled against the Lord. They are to lift up their hearts and hands to the Lord. The devastation is immense, leaving the people wailing and treated like filth and rubbish, like someone in a deep pit. The speaker, however, calls upon the Lord from the bottom of the pit. The Lord tells the speaker not to fear. The speaker calls upon the Lord to witness his disgrace and ridicule in the sight of the enemy and to pursue and totally destroy them.

Chapter 4 follows the tone of chapters 1 and 2 in speaking of the misery of Judah during the siege. The poet writes of gold losing its luster, which is a reference to the children who are treated like clay jugs, pottery that is tossed away when broken. The thirst of the people is so great, the tongue of the infant sticks to the roof of the mouth. Their suffering is greater than that of Sodom, which the Lord destroyed in an instant with no human hand causing its annihilation. The people, who once were healthy and beautiful and who lived in luxury, are now blacker than soot with their flesh clinging to their bones. Those who endure the physical onslaughts of the sword or bleeding wounds are better off than those who must endure the pangs and weakness of hunger. The people practice the worst type of cannibalism as mothers boil their young.

No king or inhabitants of the earth believed an enemy could overtake Jerusalem, but the Lord abandoned the city because of the sins of the prophets and priests who shed the blood of the just. The prophets and priests stumble blindly, polluted with so much blood the people treat them like lepers who are considered untouchable and outcasts from the community. The Lord used to protect them, but the Lord now shows no regard for the priests and elders.

In verse 17 and the following, the poet joins himself to the suffering people. The poet and the people search in vain for help, looking from the watchtower for help from another nation, most likely referring to the hoped-for help from Egypt. The enemy moves faster than eagles, pursuing them through the mountains and the wilderness. The people flee to other nations, hoping to find rest and acceptance, but they are caught in the snares set up by the nations. The land of Edom (the northern tribe of Israel) will experience the cup of wrath poured out on Judah and will be stripped naked of all their people and treasures. In the same way, the Lord will lay bare the sins of the people of Zion.

In chapter 5, the poet again calls upon the Lord to witness the disgrace of the community. Their homes are possessed by strangers, their population overridden with orphans and widows. To obtain food, the people must ally themselves with Egypt and Assyria and expose themselves to the heat of the desert. They must even pay to use the water and wood produced in their own land. They are experiencing the punishment meant for their ancestors who sinned. The armies of the enemy rule over them with no one strong enough to free them.

The enemy rapes their women, hangs their princes, treats the elders disrespectfully, and forces their youth to carry staggering loads of wood. Music and joy have left the city. The people question why the Lord has abandoned them for so long, and they beg the Lord to take them back. They concede the Lord has totally abandoned them.

### Lectio Divina

Spend 8 to 10 minutes in silent contemplation of the following passage:

One of the most difficult facts of life to understand is the fact of suffering in the world. In the midst of suffering, the one who laments experiences the greatest challenge to faith. Where is the Lord who allows such a dismal situation as that in Judah? The one who offers the third lament says nothing about abandoning the Lord or losing faith. The lament offers an example of keeping faith in the midst of the greatest form of suffering and tragedy in life.

✠ *What can I learn from this passage?*

## Day 2: The Letter to Jerusalem (Baruch 1:1—3:8)

Baruch, living in exile in Babylon, wrote his scroll in the fifth year, on the seventh day, of the year 587 BC, the day the Chaldeans destroyed Jerusalem with fire. He reads the scroll in the presence of Jeconiah, the king of Judah, and all the people in exile. As Baruch reads his scroll, the people weep, fast, and pray before the Lord. According to the text, the people—for the sake of procuring burnt offerings, sin offerings, and frankincense for offerings on the altar of the Lord for the life of Nebuchadnezzar and his son, Belshazzar—sent funds to Jerusalem. Belshazzar was not actually the son of Nebuchadnezzar and never a king, but he was the son of the last king of Babylon named Nabonidus.

About ten months after the events in the first four verses of the Book of Baruch, Baruch received vessels removed from the Temple by Nebuchadnezzar. These silver vessels, which Baruch was to restore to Judah, were made after Nebuchadnezzar took King Jeconiah, the princes, the skilled workers, the nobles, and the people of the land from Jerusalem to Babylon.

The following section (1:5—3:8) is based largely on the Book of Daniel (9:4–15), which is an admission of guilt and the sinfulness of the people. The scroll declares that from the time of Moses to the present, the people sinned and refused to listen to the Word of the Lord. It recalls warnings given by the Lord against the judges, kings, princes, and people of Israel and Judah. In the Book of Deuteronomy, Moses predicted a nation would lay siege to the land of the Israelites, causing them to eat their own sons and daughters, with each one unwilling to share this flesh with others, even those close to them (see Deuteronomy 28:49–57). The scroll identifies the Israelites as an object of revulsion and horror among all the nations.

The message of the scroll prays that the Lord, who once led the people out of Egypt "with signs and wonders and great might," will withdraw all anger from the people who have committed sacrilege against the Lord (2:11). Baruch prays that the Lord will deliver them from bondage so the whole world will recognize the God of Israel as the true Lord of all. He pleads with the Lord, saying it is not the dead who will proclaim the glory of the Lord but the truly repentant and weak person who is bowed down and feeble, with failing eyes and a famished soul, who will proclaim glory and justice for the Lord.

Baruch recalls the Lord instructed the people to serve the king of Babylon in order to preserve the land the Lord gave their ancestors, and he warns that if the people do not obey, joy and gladness shall no longer be heard in the land. The people suffered terribly and died, as predicted, by the sword, famine, and plague. The house of Judah and Israel was reduced to what it became in the exile.

Baruch also recalls a message from Moses that declared if the people would not listen to the Word of the Lord, then the numerous mass of the people will dwindle in the nations to which the Lord scatters them. In the land of exile, the Lord will give them a listening heart, leading them to praise the Lord in the land of their exile. The Lord will bring them back to the land promised on oath to Abraham, Isaac, and Jacob, and they will increase. The Lord will establish an eternal covenant with them, and the

Lord will be their God, and they will be the Lord's people (see Leviticus 26:27–46). Baruch prays that the Lord will look with compassion upon their wretched condition and the punishment they are enduring for all the sinful deeds of their ancestors.

### Lectio Divina

Spend 8 to 10 minutes in silent contemplation of the following passage:

Baruch dares to pray that the Lord will forgive the people, despite their sins. Jesus offers encouraging words to sinners when he says, "I tell you, there will be rejoicing among the angels of God over one sinner who repents" (Luke 15:10). God is compassionate and forgiving.

✠ *What can I learn from this passage?*

_____

## Day 3: In Praise of Wisdom (3:9—4:4)

Baruch questions why Israel is in the land of the enemy, counted among those destined for death, and he answers his own question, telling his people they have forsaken the fountain of wisdom. If they followed the law of the Lord, they would have had enduring peace. They should learn that prudence, strength, and understanding exist in the Word of the Lord.

Baruch points out the foolishness of seeking earthly treasures that cannot provide a long, healthy, and peaceful life. Where are those who foolishly ruled over nations and lorded over the animals? Where are those who hoarded silver, gold, and possessions? Baruch answers that they died, and others have taken their place. Later generations have come, still lacking understanding and wisdom. The people of Canaan, Teman, the descendants of Hagar, the merchants of Medan and Tema, the storytellers, and those seeking knowledge all lack the path to true wisdom.

Baruch speaks to Israel about how far the Lord's dominion stretches: vast, endless, high, and immeasurable. Giants were born in the Lord's dominion, but the Lord did not give them a path to understanding. The Book of Genesis speaks of a tribe of giants named the Nephilim who did not survive the Flood in Noah's day (see Genesis 6:4–13). No one has "gone up to the heavens" or traveled the seas to seek and obtain wisdom (3:29). No one knows the way except "he who knows all things," who created all things, the Master who makes the stars shine, and the stars respond with joy (3:32–35). No one can compare with the Lord God.

The Lord has opened the way of understanding to Jacob, the servant of the Lord, whom the Lord loves. Through the descendants of Jacob, wisdom has appeared on earth and resides with mortals. Baruch says wisdom is the book of the decrees of the Lord, a law that endures forever. Those who follow her will live, while those who forsake her will die. He calls on the descendants of Jacob to walk in the light of wisdom, not relinquishing her to foreign nations. The Lord has blessed Israel in allowing the nation to know what is pleasing to the Lord.

### Lectio Divina

Spend 8 to 10 minutes in silent contemplation of the following passage:

In the Book of Sirach, the author speaks of Wisdom as a person who comes forth from the mouth of God and covers the earth like a mist (see Sirach 24:3). Wisdom leads to faith, understanding, hope, and love. In the Old Testament, we read Wisdom made her dwelling with the descendants of Jacob (see Sirach 24:8). Jesus speaks of Wisdom as the Holy Spirit when he says the Holy Spirit "will teach you everything and remind you of all that I told you" (John 14:26). Faith and understanding come from Wisdom, the Holy Spirit.

✠ *What can I learn from this passage?*

---

## Day 4: Poem of Consolation (Baruch 4:5—5:9)

Baruch calls upon the exiles to be courageous, reminding them the Lord sold them to their enemies, not for their destruction but as a result of their abandonment of the Lord. They angered their Maker by offering sacrifices to demons in place of God. Zion, speaking as though a person, tells her neighbors God brought great sorrow upon her who witnessed the captivity of her sons and daughters. She nurtured her people and lamented when she sent them away, making her like a sorrowful and abandoned widow. Because her children turned away from the Lord and refused to follow the Lord's statutes, she was left desolate. The Lord brought upon them a far-away nation of ruthless invaders who spoke an alien language and lacked respect for old age or for children. Zion bids farewell to her sons and daughters, exchanging her garment of peace for a garment of sackcloth, crying out to the Eternal One.

Zion hopes in the Lord, trusting the Lord will bring her children back to her. Just as the nation's neighbors saw the people of Zion taken captive, they will soon witness the freedom that the Lord bestows on the nation. They will see the salvation that will clearly demonstrate the glory and splendor of the Eternal One. Zion encourages her children to bear God's wrath patiently, for they will soon trample on the necks of their enemy. Now is the time to turn their hearts to the Lord who once brought them disaster and will bring them to the eternal joy of freedom.

Baruch speaks of the disaster in store for the nation who brought the Israelites into captivity. Just as the nation rejoiced when Jerusalem fell, so now she shall grieve over her own destruction. Fire shall come upon her from the Eternal One and demons shall inhabit her for a long time. Baruch invites Jerusalem to look to the east and west to see her returning children, rejoicing in the glory of the Lord. He directs her to trade her robe of mourning for the splendor and glory of God, who shall wrap her in a mantle of justice and place a diadem of glory on her head. The imagery reflects a sharing in the royalty of the Lord. Following the custom of the day by which a new name is given to someone starting a new beginning, the Lord adds a new name to Jerusalem, calling her "the peace of justice, the glory of God's worship" (5:4). The return of the children of Jerusalem shall be smooth, with mountains laid low and valleys filled. At the command of the Lord, the forests and fragrant plants will shade Israel and the light of the Lord's glory will lead the Israelites.

## Lectio Divina

Spend 8 to 10 minutes in silent contemplation of the following passage:

In the aftermath of forest fires or floods that destroy homes, we often hear people utter the same words, "We'll just have to rebuild." Undaunted by the devastation, many people have the courage to enter a new phase of life, looking to the future rather than allowing the past to destroy them. The same happens with the Israelites in exile. A remnant will return to their devastated land and declare,

"We'll just have to rebuild," which is what they did. Resurrection is part of living.

✠ *What can I learn from this passage?*

---

## Day 5: The Letter of Jeremiah (6)

The letter of Jeremiah was a much later addition to the Book of Baruch and was not written by Jeremiah. The theme of the letter centers on the emptiness of idol worship and the warnings against idol worship. The opening line of the letter claims to be a copy of the letter that Jeremiah sent to the Israelites captive in exile in Babylon, telling them their sins led them into captivity. The author predicts the Lord will bring them back from Babylon after seven generations have passed. The number seven here is most likely meant to be a symbolic number and should not be taken literally.

The author belittles the worship of idols, describing the idols as the work of artisans who decorate their images with gold and silver and adorn the images like an elegantly dressed girl. The people bring gold and silver for the idols that the priests steal for their own personal use or for a harlot in a brothel. The idols rust and corrode like any other metal. Each one has an ax or dagger in its right hand, but it cannot save itself from pillage or war. Since they are not gods, there is no need to fear them.

The author continues to speak of the emptiness of the images. They are as useless as a broken pot, covered with dust, and stand well protected with walls, gates, bars, and bolts so that robbers will not steal them. They are like the timber in the Temple, with crawling creatures consuming them and their garments without them feeling it. Bats, birds, and cats climb over them. Since they are not gods, there is no need to fear them.

Gold adorns the images, but someone must wipe away the corrosion to make them shine. Since they cannot walk, they must be carried shoulder high, and if they fall, someone must pick them up. Ritually unclean women handle their sacrifices. From these practices, recognize that they are not gods, so do not fear them.

The false gods cannot give riches, save people from death, make the weak strong, restore sight to the blind, or rescue anyone in distress. They have no pity for the widow or orphan, and their silver and gold statues are no better than stones from the mountain.

When the Chaldeans encounter a deaf mute, they senselessly bring the god Bel for healing. Women, with cords around them, sit by the road burning chaff for incense. When one is taken aside for prostitution, she returns and mocks those whose cord has not been broken. The unbroken cord is a sign this woman was unworthy of serving a man. At times of war, the priests try to hide with these gods to save themselves from war or disaster, a sure sign these images are not gods. They do not set up kings or bring rain. They cannot resist an invading king or enemy forces. In a fire, they burn up while the priests scurry to save themselves. The prophet retorts, "How then can it be thought or claimed that they are gods?" (6:39).

It is much better to be a valiant king, a handy tool in a house, a door to the house, or a wooden post in a palace, all of which have a function. Like lightning, wind, clouds, fire, and forests—which carry out the command of the Lord—these are more beautiful and powerful than the false gods, who cannot judge or benefit anyone.

False idols cannot curse or bless kings. They do not shine like the sun or give light like the moon. Unlike beasts who run for shelter when needed, the idols cannot help themselves. In no way is it apparent these idols are gods, so do not fear them. False idols are like a scarecrow in a cucumber field or like a thornbush on which birds perch. The just who do not possess idols are better off. They will avoid all shame.

### Lectio Divina

When someone believes the person he or she is speaking to is not listening, he often uses the expression, "I might as well be speaking to the wall." The author of the Letter of Jeremiah has no doubt speaking to idols is as productive as speaking to the wall. At times when we pray, we may feel like we are speaking to the wall, but God is always listening, and something is happening, even if we don't see it. We worship with faith a loving and concerned God.

✠ *What can I learn from this passage?*

## Review Questions

1. What are some of the miseries encountered by Jerusalem when it was under siege?

2. Why does the author of Baruch refer to living under the king of Babylon as though he were a protective hand?

3. What does the author mean when he says Wisdom is at home with humans?